KILLING OF A LEGEND

Mickey Thompson Double Murders

By Ronald E Bowers
Former Senior Prosecutor
Los Angeles County District Attorney's Office

Some names and locations have been changed to protect the privacy of individuals connected with this story. Certain events have been inferred from the facts of these cases. Some quotes and dialogue have been changed for brevity.

Ronald E. Bowers, Publisher
losangelestruecrime@aol.com

ISBN 978-1-7325281-5-4

Second release February 2017

INTRODUCTION

On March 16, 1988, I, the author, was the Head Deputy in charge of the Norwalk DA's Office, which handled mainly all the prosecution of cases for the Southeast section of Los Angeles County. The Norwalk Branch of the DA's Office had a reputation for being the toughest in the County. Criminal Defense attorneys hated the place, claiming the DA's Office didn't have a 'WELCOME' mat out for them. I lived 25 miles from this Norwalk Office and had to endure a lengthy commute on some of the busiest freeways in the County. At 6:05 a.m., I was still at home just finishing showering, shaving, and getting myself ready for another hectic drive to work. By 7:00 a.m., I was out the door and on the road headed to the Norwalk courthouse.

It was a nondescript day, slightly overcast, nothing a diarist would find interesting to write about. Since it was a long drive, I turned on the radio and enjoyed the banter of the morning DJs, discussing nothing of significance that had occurred previously on this March 16th day. By checking history, the most important event to befall on this day was in 1916: the U.S. Cavalry, under the command of John Pershing, crossed the US–Mexican border to join in the hunt for Pancho Villa. (That wasn't all that exciting, except to trivia buffs.)

By 8:15 a.m. I had pulled into the Head Deputy parking space at the Norwalk courthouse and proceeded up to my office on the second floor of the building. I entered my office as I had done hundreds of time before, and hung my coat on what was called a 'hat rack.' (In the 1980s no one wore hats, but every office in a county building had an aging 'hat rack.') Then I sat down behind my oversized county desk and glanced at the daily court calendar to see what cases might require special attention. I had an 'Open Door Policy,' which meant the attorneys and staff could feel free to enter and talk to me about any issues or questions they may have. Since my door was open, a Sheriff's deputy popped his head in. He said, "Mr. Bowers, have you heard Mickey Thompson has been shot?"

I responded, "What are you talking about?" At that time the deputy stepped into my office and stated, "I just heard from the Sheriff's station that Mickey Thompson and his wife were shot to death at their Bradbury home." I tried to process all the information. My initial thought was how certain was he that it was the same Mickey Thompson who had broken the speed record at Bonneville Salt Flats.

As a teenager, I enjoyed working on cars. The name Mickey Thompson was always talked about for his racing achievements. He was a 'Man's man,' accomplishing things that no one else had ever done. I don't know if it was his willingness to push boundaries or his business acumen that fascinated me the most about him. Mickey always seemed larger than life. His image and name were always being seen on TV announcing Motocross events at Anaheim Stadium or a tire commercial for Mickey Thompson all-terrain tires.

I asked the Sheriff's deputy how certain he was that the victim was the legendary Mickey Thompson. I don't know whether I was in denial or just trying to be cautious. To me, the name Mickey Thompson was a very common name, so maybe it was really someone else. As a matter of fact, there was a local Mike Thompson RV sales business that was always advertising on TV. The deputy didn't know how to respond to my doubts. As he started walking out of my office, he said he would call the station to verify the facts of the shooting.

Whenever I was in doubt about something, I would check with my secretary, since she had a better grasp as to what was going on in the building. Pushing my chair aside, I got up and walked over to her office. As I approached, I could hear a radio playing what sounded like 'Man in the Mirror' by Michael Jackson, which at that time was number one on the charts. My secretary always listened to so-called 'elevator music' on her little transistor radio. As I was looking for her, an announcer came on the radio and in an excited voice stated he was reporting from the City of Bradbury. I stopped to listen more carefully to what he was announcing. He said, "Sheriff's Homicide stated that they were conducting an investigation into the deaths of two victims at the Mickey Thompson residence."

We weren't told initially as to the identification of the victims, but now I had the verification I needed to accept the chilling news that I had earlier found hard to accept. When the deputy Sheriff returned to my office, he provided more details about the shooting. He mentioned that Sgt. Ray Verdugo was one of the homicide detectives assigned to the case. That gave me a sense of relief and confidence that the investigation would be thorough, since I personally knew the detective. Years earlier, I had worked with Ray Verdugo on a case in which I prosecuted a defendant, Juan Gonzalez, who had shot and killed Deputy Jack Williams who was serving a search warrant at Gonzalez's house.

I had handled many narcotics cases with the victim Deputy Jack Williams. He was a real salt-of-the-earth type of person. He wasn't a BS'er but a conscientious narcotics deputy. I liked Jack, and when he was murdered his case by happenstance was assigned to me. That was when I worked closely with Sgt. Verdugo to see what could be done to vigorously prosecute the killer. As a result, I became acquainted with Verdugo and his thorough approach to solving homicides.

With the assurance of knowing that Sgt. Verdugo, as well as a crew of Sheriff's Homicide detectives, was on the Mickey Thompson case, I was confident it would soon be solved. Life went on for me and my family. I became preoccupied with my career, trying to navigate my way up the ladder in the chain of command at the DA's Office. The Mickey Thompson case became a vague memory. I assumed the detectives were close to resolving the case, but time marched on without any arrests being announced.

Eventually, my daughter, Julianna, started horseback riding lessons at a riding school in the City of Bradbury. As many parents learn when raising a young teenage daughter, there is a perpetual question that comes up between father and daughter as to why your daughter's friends have their own horses, and your loving daughter doesn't have one. The easiest way to address that inequality is by enrolling your daughter in a horseback riding school. So that is what my wife and I did. As it turned out, the nearest riding school for her age group was in Bradbury.

Every time I drove her for a lesson in Bradbury, I had to pass through a security gatehouse and be checked out before I could enter through the city gates. When I drove through, I pondered how the two killers in the Thompson case could have been able to get into Bradbury without being detected. Every time I drove my daughter down the narrow lanes and passed by the large country estates, I had the feeling that the Bradbury residents had to be living in their own little Camelot. You could see the young people riding their horses down the horse trails where everything looked so tranquil in this diminutive enclave. The children had smiling faces, waving to passersby, while residents congregated on street corners socializing. Everyone knew each other and seemed to have a common bond revolving around their love for horses.

All the years my daughter took horseback riding lessons in Bradbury, I wondered just where the Thompsons' estate was located. I knew it was on the eastern border of the city; however, I always entered on the west side and never had an occasion to drive by their house. Time continued to march by and I didn't hear much about the investigation. I remember my son, Jeff, going to a Motocross show at Anaheim Stadium. He was so excited to see the quads and motorcycles race on the dirt-filled stadium floor. The revving of the engines, the whiff of exhaust fumes, and the colorfully painted racecars were all circling the track at breakneck speeds. The advertisement for these races always mentioned the founder of the event, Mickey Thompson.

As months turned into years, still no arrests had been made for the double murders that had captivated the interest of the country many years before. Over the next 13 years, little was reported about the case or any mention as to the investigation. The only reference to the Mickey Thompson case was when *America's Most Wanted* would do an updated TV program about the case. They showed a Wanted Poster with a composite drawing of the two blacks who had been identified as the shooters. Approximately every five years another TV program would do a re-enactment of the shooting asking for the public's help in solving these cruel, malicious murders.

By the late 1990s, pressure was mounting on the Sheriff's Department to reopen the Thompson investigation. There is a myth often repeated by law enforcement that claims that no homicide case is ever closed until it is solved. The real reason for this is that the statute of limitation never runs out on murder cases. However, in the real world, homicide cases go to the Cold Case files when there are no more workable leads. Technically, this means the case is still 'open,' but no one is actually working on it on a daily basis.

Mickey and his sister, Colleen Campbell, both grew up in the City of Alhambra. Their father, Marion Lee 'Tommy' Thompson, was the head of detectives and eventually became the Police Chief of Alhambra. In the 1970s I had been promoted to the first Deputy in Charge of the Alhambra DA's Office. Although the Thompson family had moved away from Alhambra, I was aware of the influence the Thompson family had on the Alhambra Police Department.

Mickey's sister, Mrs. Campbell, had been the mayor of San Juan Capistrano, and she was well aware of how things got done. When pressure is exerted on the right group of people, things are looked into. She knew how to apply pressure to encourage the Sheriff's Department to once again look into the homicide of her brother, Mickey, and his wife, Trudy. She was also able to convince the Los Angeles County Sheriff's Department to assign a new detective to the aging 13-year-old case. She wanted fresh eyes to review it. I don't know the details of what pressure was applied, but the LA County Sheriff's Department did assign one of their most tenacious homicide detectives to the case. His name was Detective Mark Lillienfeld and he was well known in his own right as an energetic, persistent detective who was extremely creative and, could be described as shrewd.

Det. Lillienfeld had been involved in solving some of the toughest cases confronting the Sheriff's Department, and he had earned a reputation for getting his man. One could say that a legendary detective had been assigned to solve the murder of the legendary Mickey Thompson. Mickey's sister believed that it was Mickey's old business partner who was behind the murders. When Mickey was trying to slow down his business activities, he had looked for a partner, and that was when Michael Goodwin entered the picture. They formed a partnership that didn't work out and was quickly dissolved within months. What resulted was one of the bitterest lawsuits and hotly contested cases ever to pass through the American Court System.

Det. Lillienfeld, not surprisingly, zeroed in on Michael Goodwin as the mastermind who had hired two black men to kill Mickey and Trudy. The public didn't receive much new information about this case, except for the possibility that Det. Lillienfeld had found eyewitnesses who claimed they saw a man scoping out Mickey's place just two days before the shooting. Even though it was 13 years later, one of these witnesses was able to identify Goodwin's photo out of six photos shown to him. The detectives then needed to hold a live lineup to see if this witness could really pick him out. When the detectives asked Goodwin to appear in such a lineup, he refused and took the Sheriff's Department to court to prevent this.

I didn't pay much attention to this new revelation in which Goodwin was identified by two people in a live lineup as being seen in the area several days before the murders. Since the killings occurred in Bradbury, which is clearly a part of Los Angeles County, I waited to see when the case would be brought to the LA District Attorney's Office. However, I was surprised when it was announced that the Orange County DA's Office had filed Conspiracy to Murder charges against Goodwin. I wondered why this had happened and learned that some of the acts of the Conspiracy to Murder had occurred in Orange County. There was a claim that the murder weapons and possibly a stun gun had been purchased in Orange County by Goodwin.

I was pleased that charges had been brought against Goodwin, even though the court proceeding occurred in Orange County. To me, this would provide closure for the Thompson family. The Goodwin case continued to percolate through the Orange County court system, and it was only a matter of time before the case would be history.

Then, one day several years later, there was an announcement on TV that the California Appellate Court had ruled that Orange County wasn't the proper venue for filing the Goodwin case. That came as a shock to me since I had compartmentalized this in my mind as a closed matter. I wondered what this all meant, since it appeared that originally the LADA's Office had rejected the case. The court set a date by which, if no new charges were filed in the proper venue (Los Angeles County), Goodwin had to be released.

In my mind, that meant that Mickey's killer was getting away with murder. This, to me, was very discouraging, but I had seen other criminals go unpunished for their crimes. I continued working for the DA's Office and paid no attention to the Mickey Thompson case.

About two weeks later, the Head Deputy of Major Crimes Division, Pat Dixon, came into my office and said, "Ron, I have someone in my office I want you to meet." So I dropped what I was working on and followed Pat to his huge corner office. He walked behind his desk and sat down. Pat didn't believe in cleaning his desk but was one of those so-called 'stacker people' who continually stacks new items on top of the layers of law books and case files that have accumulated over the years. I remained standing; waiting to see what this was all about.

I noticed another man standing to the side of Pat's cluttered desk. He was medium in stature with a huge smile and was wearing a suit that was slightly too tight. He reminded me of an old-time encyclopedia salesman. (The internet has eliminated that occupation.) Pat said, "Ron, this is Det. Mark Lillienfeld from Sheriff's Homicide." He leaned toward me and we shook hands. I had heard about Det. Lillienfeld but had never met him.

My mind was racing at 100 mph questioning why I was in this meeting with Det. Lillienfeld. Pat started out saying that Mark was the lead detective in the Michael Goodwin case. Then Pat said, "I want you to work with Det. Lillienfeld to prepare a PowerPoint presentation for me to give to the District Attorney and Administrative staff explaining what evidence exists for prosecuting the Michael Goodwin case."

I didn't say anything. I had heard from the news media that Goodwin was going to be released soon from custody. I was then told there wasn't much time to get all this together, but I was to stop working on any other cases and concentrate all my efforts on this presentation for the DA.

My response was, "Okay, where's the evidence?" Det. Lillienfeld said that he would get the boxes of reports and documents from the Orange County DA's Office and have them delivered to my office. I tried to explain that I couldn't do much on the presentation until I had this material. That was when the true legend of Det.

Lillienfeld came alive. He said, with a Cheshire cat grin, **"Ron, don't worry, all the reports will be in your office by noon tomorrow."** I had only known Det. Lillienfeld less than 15 minutes and we were on a first name basis. Here was someone who had a high degree of confidence that he could control things going on around him. If I had been him, I would have said, "I will try to get you all the material if I can find a mover who is available." As an attorney, I would have inserted some form of a disclaimer if for some reason I was unable to deliver as promised.

The next day I was busily trying to finish up on the other cases I had been working on, then I left for an early lunch to beat the crowd at the sandwich shop. By 12:15p.m., I returned to my office, and as I stepped in I abruptly stopped, thinking I had entered the wrong office. The entire west wall of my office was piled to the ceiling with file boxes. Several of the boxes had written on the outside of them the word 'GOODWIN.' I looked at the desk and recognized it was mine. As I squeezed by the stacks of boxes, I was able to negotiate myself to my chair and plunk myself down. I saw a note scribbled on a sheet of paper from a yellow legal tablet lying on top of all my papers on my desk. It said, "Ron, you said you wanted the material on the Mickey Thompson case. Well, you got it. Now put together a great PowerPoint on it." It was hard to make out the scribbled signature, but it didn't matter, I knew that it was from the one and only **Mark Lillienfeld**. From that point on, I never questioned Mark's resolve. If he said that he would do certain things, I knew I could take that promise to the bank.

From where I sat I couldn't count the number of boxes, but it was somewhere between 20 and 30. Now I realized Mark had hit the ball into my court. So what was I going to do? I was beginning to experience a sinking feeling. I had asked for all the material, but I never actually thought it would all be dumped in my office. As I gazed at the wall of boxes, I thought there must be some order to them. But there were no numbers written on the outside of the boxes to indicate any special order.

I rose from my chair and reached for the nearest box on the top of the stack. I pulled off the lid and there were various records of the business partnership between Mickey and Goodwin. I quickly slammed the lid back on and reached for another box. That one had reports and documents about Goodwin and his wife leaving the country shortly after the shooting. As I closed up that box, I recalled the old bit from Laurel and Hardy comedies in which Hardy would look at Laurel and say, "Here's another fine kettle of fish you've got us into." I had never in my wildest thoughts believed I would be so deeply involved in this case. I thought to myself, OK let's get started and see if all this mountain of evidence can build a case against Michael Goodwin.

This introduction is meant to explain why and how I know about the facts of the Mickey Thompson case. Some readers are disappointed that True Crime authors don't provide insight from all sides, including both the Prosecution and the Defense. What the reader has to understand is that the author has access to only certain evidence when viewing a case. My only access is from the prosecution side. I didn't have any access to the Defense side of the case; therefore, I can't discuss information I'm not privy to. To those critics who will say this book has a 'prosecution slant,' all I can say is I am sorry, but I can't write a True Crime story about something I wasn't a part of. Nonetheless, I still believe this book provides you, the public, with valuable insight as to how our Criminal Justice System really works.

The following chapters reflect what I have learned over a two-year period in which I tried to make sense out of 15 years of investigative reports, documents, photos, and interviews. When I started sifting through the material, I realized one important thing was the need to identify the **irrelevant** evidence and cast it aside. Then identify the **relevant** evidence and start connecting the dots between the various pieces. The secret to this case was conveying only the evidence the jury needed to know and avoiding the path where you get lost in the weeds. After all those years, there were plenty of tall weeds that had grown to obscure the viewing of the incriminating facts.

CONTENTS

CHAPTER 1. Leaving for Work 1

CHAPTER 2. The Shooting (March 16, 1988, at 6:10 a.m.) 7

CHAPTER 3. Life in Bradbury 11

CHAPTER 4. Killers Escaping 15

CHAPTER 5. Witnesses to the Shooting..21

CHAPTER 6. Witnesses to the Escape...27

CHAPTER 7. Looking for Crime Scene Evidence..33

CHAPTER 8. Investigation of the Ex-Partner..41

CHAPTER 10. Who Was Mickey Thompson?...51

CHAPTER 11. Breaking Records...55

CHAPTER 12. Business Ventures 61

CHAPTER 13. Meeting Trudy...65

CHAPTER 14. Michael Goodwin the Promoter..71

CHAPTER 15. Partnership Is Formed 75

CHAPTER 16. Dissolving of Partnership..79

CHAPTER 17. Bitter Lawsuit 81

CHAPTER 19. Leaving the Country...91

CHAPTER 20. Goodwin Returns to USA..97

CHAPTER 22. New Witnesses Surface 107

CHAPTER 23. Lineup of Goodwin 111

CHAPTER 24. Goodwin Threats 117
CHAPTER 25. Orange County's Involvement 125
CHAPTER 26. Orange County Filed Charges 129
CHAPTER 27. Orange County Proceedings 133
CHAPTER 28. Los Angeles County DA Decision 137
CHAPTER 29. LADA's Office Strategy 147
CHAPTER 30. Preliminary Hearing 151
CHAPTER 31. Checking Out Crime Scene 159
CHAPTER 32. Finally the Trial Begins 165
CHAPTER 33. DA's Opening Statement 169
CHAPTER 34. Defense Opening Statement 177
CHAPTER 35. DA's Evidence at Trial 183
CHAPTER 36. Defense Evidence at Trial 193
CHAPTER 37. Jury Field Trip 199
CHAPTER 38. DA's Argument 205
CHAPTER 39. Defense's Argument 215
CHAPTER 40. Verdict & Sentencing 221
CHAPTER 41. EPILOGUE 229

CHAPTER 1. LEAVING FOR WORK

During the morning hours of Tuesday, March 16th of 1988, Mickey (59) and Trudy (41) Thompson hurried around their Bradbury home readying themselves for work. Mickey didn't want to be late and Trudy, his wife, couldn't convince him that there was no reason to rush, especially since he was the boss and didn't need to impress anyone. For whatever reason, Mickey had embedded in his character the necessity of promptness. Was it his old Marine background, or was it his upbringing as the son of a police chief? Mickey confirmed the old saying: "Early to bed, early to rise, makes a man healthy, wealthy, and wise." Mickey believed that "early risers" would enjoy good health, acquire abundant wealth, and certainly possess wisdom in their business endeavors.

He scurried into the attached garage with Trudy trailing close behind. Mickey had been procrastinating in fixing their remote control garage door opener. In order to get the garage door to open, he had to use the button next to the side door in the back of the garage. Standing in the door frame, he leaned over to push the garage door button. Instantly the old wooden garage door creaked as the opener's motor strained to raise the garage door all the way up. At the same time, Trudy navigated her way through the packed garage containing all the timeworn racing mementos that had accumulated over the years.

Trudy was able to open the driver's door to the minivan, and as she got in she turned to Mickey and in her most persuasive voice said, "Mickey, you need to get someone to fix the opener." For over a week Mickey couldn't get the remote control device to work from inside the car. He first thought it was a weak battery, but after putting new ones in it still didn't work. Mickey also tried to clean the contact points on the remote, but still no results.

Mickey didn't like to be reminded he couldn't fix a lousy remote control but he nodded his approval to his wife. By that time, Trudy was seated in the minivan and had started the engine. With the March chilly weather, she gunned the engine twice to make sure it was warmed up sufficiently for its daily trek to Anaheim Stadium where their office was located. Why was a wealthy, famous couple driving a small Toyota minivan when their prestigious Lincoln Continental sat idly by only a few feet away? Anyone who truly knew Mickey would understand this dichotomy. In Mickey's world, there was no need to flaunt one's success. Mickey didn't have to try to impress anyone, although it was important to him to be respected. He was exceedingly well grounded.

To Mickey, the idea of using the minivan sent a message to his employees and associates that thriftiness was a virtue practiced even by their wealthy boss. That wasn't to say that Mickey on weekends didn't enjoy pulling up to public events or country clubs in his Mark III Lincoln Continental. Mickey was one of the best showmen of all times and possessed some of the enduring qualities of P.T. Barnum and Buffalo Bill as master promoters and entertainers. Those showmen had figured out what the public wanted to see and they learned how to provide it.

As the minivan proceeded to back out of the garage, Mickey could see the first rays of sunlight coming through the lanky eucalyptus trees that swayed from a mild breeze. With the garage door fully open, he could feel a slight nip from the early morning air. Mickey, as though in automatic mode, pressed the button to close the garage door. As he waited for the door to descend, his eyes gazed throughout his garage, which was filled with all sorts of racing souvenirs and keepsakes that he had stored while waiting for that rainy day to organize it for some display purpose. He had hopes that shortly he would have more time as he tried to wind down his racing business, but all the garage clutter would have to wait for another day. As he spun around and walked out the back door he was wondering how he could be the fastest man on wheels, but yet he couldn't get his garage door remote control to work.

He slammed closed the garage's side door and locked it. With that, he walked around the back of the garage in order to join Trudy in the minivan. He felt fortunate that it wasn't raining as he rounded the corner. He could look down on his huge stable barn that he had converted into a giant auto shop. Maybe this weekend he would take the garage opener down to his shop and figure out what was wrong with it.

It wasn't the cost of paying someone to fix it that concerned him; it was that he had always enjoyed the challenge of trying to make things work. When he was a kid growing up in Alhambra, California, about ten miles away from Bradbury, he could take a junky old automobile and convert it into an amazing racing machine. He had a knack for fixing things. He would test out his overpowered hot rods on the city streets. On many occasions, he would roar around the streets while the cops in town would look the other way since his dad was the Police Chief.

As Mickey came around the side of the garage, he could see Trudy waiting in the minivan at the top of their steep driveway. He and his wife were ready to take on another day, as they had done hundreds of times before. It was 6:05 a.m. and all was well in Mickey's world. Mickey was so predictable one could set their watch on his behavior. Unfortunately, that foreseeability was about to prove deadly for the Thompsons.

(The next graphic page shows the Thompson house with their two cars: a Lincoln and a Toyota minivan.)

Graphic 1

MICKEY & TRUDY THOMPSON HOUSE

March 16, 1988 6:05 a.m.

The Thompson house was at the top of a steep driveway

Mickey's Lincoln Continental was parked in front of the house

Trudy had backed out of the garage in this Toyota minivan

CHAPTER 2. THE SHOOTING (MARCH 16, 1988, AT 6:10 A.M.)

The City of Bradbury was exceedingly serene at 6:05 a.m. The loudest noise was an occasional horse whinny, which would echo through the foothills. As Mickey turned to walk toward the minivan where Trudy sat waiting, he felt a sudden, sharp pain in his leg. Simultaneously, he heard a loud popping sound and glanced to his right to barely notice the figure of a male pointing a gun at him. His mind went into overdrive to comprehend what was happening to him. He could feel his feet buckle under his weight as he collapsed onto the asphalt driveway. Turning to look in the direction of Trudy, he could see her face frozen in fear with her hands gripping the steering wheel of the minivan.

He could scarcely make out the voice of the man with the gun, barking out some type of command in a sharp accent. What flashed through Mickey's mind was that this was some type of robbery. As he felt the piercing pain intensify, he knew he couldn't resist. If they wanted his wallet or watch, he was willing to comply with their request. Then he heard another shot, which seemed to come from the area of the minivan. It sounded like glass shattering from a car window.

From the angle he was lying on the driveway, he could hardly make out the figure of another male with a gun pointed at Trudy. The minivan lurched backward, striking a retaining wall with the sound of a collision. Then there was another loud pop, and he could see his wife, Trudy, jump out of the vehicle and turn toward the man with the gun. She begged him to stop as she darted down the driveway. Mickey shouted from the top of the hill, "Don't shoot my wife! Please don't shoot my wife." Those pleas were answered by the gunman shooting again at Trudy. After two rapid shots, she stumbled and fell to the rough driveway. That shooter wasn't far behind Trudy. She seemed to rise up but collapsed to her knees and began crawling down the driveway. She was using her hands to frantically pull herself further down toward the street.

Mickey, at the top of the driveway, crawled slightly to better see where Trudy had gone. He felt totally helpless as he stared at Trudy desperately trying to escape. Mickey could hear the two men with guns shout at each other. With their thick accents, he couldn't make out exactly what they were saying, although it sounded like the words, "Now, now." Then "OK. Do it." At which point the man moved over to where Trudy had fallen. He leaned over, holding the gun inches from her head, then fired twice at point blank range. After the second shot, Trudy's head slumped to the ground.

Mickey could see Trudy's body go limp in the gutter at the bottom of the driveway. He tried to rise up to go to her aid when he heard the sound of two shots. Within seconds, he felt nothing as the blood started gushing out of his body and his mind faded to OFF. His shooter wanted to be certain of his demise and placed the 9mm automatic next to his head and squeezed the trigger twice in rapid succession. Mickey's head pounded against the driveway and slightly bounced back up. Within seconds, his head had what looked like a halo of blood surrounding it. His body twitched slightly, and then calm came over him as he lay motionless with a steady stream of blood oozing down the driveway

At that moment in time, the ultimate pain had been inflicted on Mickey. It was uncanny that Mickey's last vision of his life was that of his beloved wife being executed. Trudy had for years been the center of his life. They personified the 'perfect married couple.' He worshiped her caring personality while she revered the luminary he had become. It seemed as if the final chapter of the Mickey Thompson legend had finally been written.

What had brought the world to this? Why was it necessary for both of them to be executed within seconds of each other? Who would be behind such a dastardly deed? Both shooters took their guns and placed them in their backpacks, and they moved quickly to the top of the driveway and reached into the brush to retrieve their bikes. As they hastily mounted their bikes, they frantically pedaled down the horse trail that leads into the quaint, peaceful City of Bradbury.

(This page shows where Mickey and Trudy Thompson were shot.)

SHOOTING OF MICKEY & TRUDY THOMPSON

March 16, 1988 6:05 a.m.

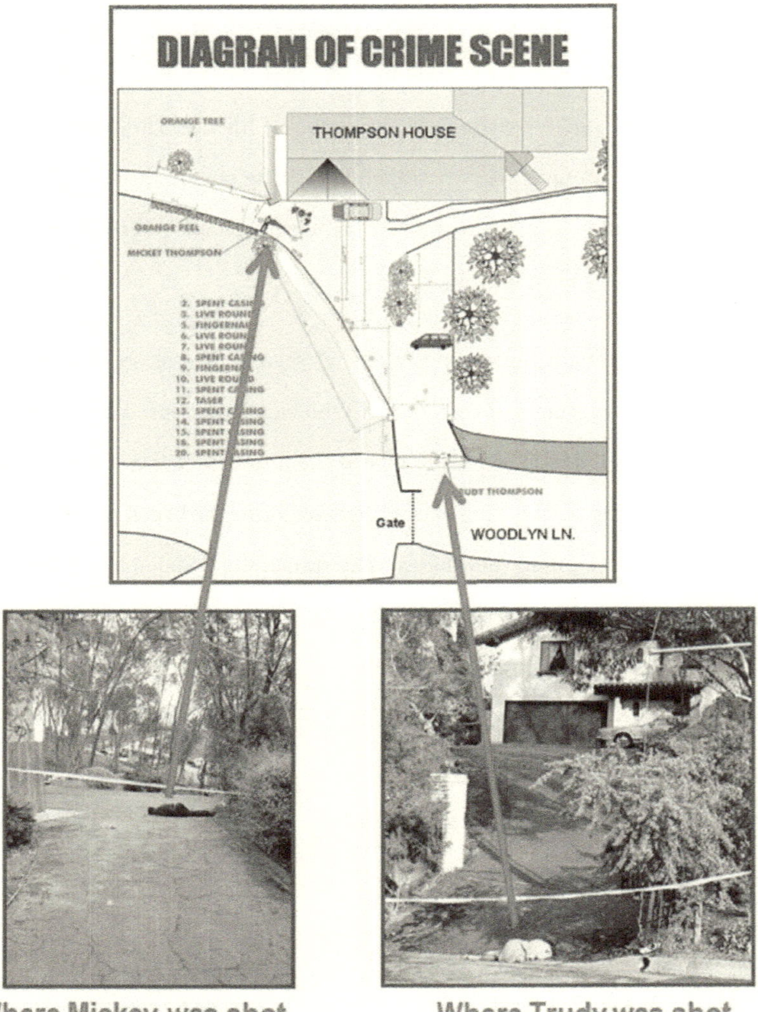

Where Mickey was shot

Where Trudy was shot

CHAPTER 3. LIFE IN BRADBURY

Life couldn't have been better for Mickey and Trudy while they lived on a huge piece of property in Bradbury. This elite gated community along the foothills is 15 miles east of the City of Los Angeles. Many consider this place to be one of the finest equestrian communities in the country. As a matter of fact, Forbes magazine placed Bradbury's zip code, 91008, as number one on its annual list of America's most expensive zip codes, with a median home price of over four million dollars. The houses are roomy, and some people might describe them as mini-mansions. Many of the residences occupy a five-acre lot and others on two-acre lots. The 'Rich and Famous' crowd who enjoy the horse world recognize Bradbury for its exclusiveness. The city motto is 'Preserving Rural Tranquility.' It combines the trappings of stables and horse show arenas within riding distance of all the houses. This isn't available for their less fortunate friends living in Beverly Hills or even Bel Air on the west side of LA The 1,048 Bradbury residents love the security of having a gated community where no riff-raff can wander about the streets. Everyone feels secure because they are safely tucked away from the child molesters, burglars, and robbers that plague many communities.

The exclusiveness feature of the community wasn't the reason Mickey and Trudy bought a home in Bradbury. Mickey thought of himself more of a Horatio Alger type who had worked his way into this affluent neighborhood by old fashion hard work. What did impress him about the neighborhood were the large lot sizes and having his house set on top of a knoll overlooking the picturesque rolling hills of the equestrian community. Mickey wasn't an equine type person, but he loved the large stable built below his property. He didn't need the barn space for horses, so he converted it into his own racing car barn. There he housed many of the special vehicles he had been working on as well as some old cars that he just liked driving on special occasions. In the end, they didn't have any horses, but he had plenty of horse power in his old restored racecars.

This was a great place to live and entertain. It was such a relaxing, laid-back setting, where the only noise was the clop clop of horseshoes as the young kids trotted their horses down the narrow country lanes. This secluded area was situated above the hustle and bustle of the busy world only half a mile below their estates. The Thompson's piece of property was situated on the eastern edge of Bradbury. One of the private gates to the community was directly below their property. Half of their property was outside the gated area and the other half enclosed in it. This was an anomaly in that they lived in Bradbury, which is mostly a gated community, but their lot was situated adjacent to a public street.

What that meant was they had the best of both worlds. Their property had a circular driveway that opened to the public streets. This was advantageous when they entertained because they didn't have to call the guard shack to provide the names of all their guests. Anyone could drive up the public street and proceed up their huge driveway. The disadvantage of this was that they didn't have complete security around their house as most of their neighbors did.

The Thompson's property was unique in that the front of the house faced a public road while the back of the house wrapped around a country lane. The actual house was high on a knoll looking down into a mini-valley area. The Triarsi family, who were witnesses to the shooting, lived just south of the Thompson house, and both houses were on the same level, elevation wise, but a ravine separated their properties.

Mickey and Trudy were well known and well-liked by their neighbors. The community consisted of some exceedingly affluent business leaders and numerous professional sports figures. Since Mickey was famous as a businessman and a sports figure, he had something in common with all the residents, with one exception: he wasn't into horses. He still was recognized as a celebrity that everyone wanted to claim they knew. Even though he enjoyed working on his racecars, he tried to keep the noise down, respecting the peacefulness of the neighborhood. Bradbury was proud to have the Thompsons as part of their rural tranquility, which makes up the city's motto.

(The next graphic page shows what the City of Bradbury looks like.)

Graphic 3

LIFE IN BRADBURY

Guardhouse

Mini-mansion

Horse Country

Many Mansion Estates

CHAPTER 4. KILLERS ESCAPING

Woodlyn Lane was the name of the road the Thompsons' house faced. That road continued for a few yards past their driveway, where there had been a gated access to the private city of Bradbury. Years earlier the community had decided to close off this street and not use it as one of the gated entrances. At that time, the wrought iron gate was permanently locked.

Trudy's body lay near that sealed-off gate at the bottom of Thompson's driveway. In her attempt to get away from the shooters, she ended up lying in the concrete gutter with her legs curled onto the public street while her head rested on the apron area of their driveway. Because of the locked gate, the two shooters couldn't escape down Woodlyn Lane. Both shooters sprinted up the driveway toward the garage. There they retrieved their two bicycles from under the tall bushes. Hastily, they jumped on the bikes and started coasting down a paved horse path on the west side of the property. They sped down the path and when they got to the bottom they merged onto Woodlyn Lane, which at that point was well inside the gated community of Bradbury. From there they hurriedly pedaled on this curvy lane that passed by several horse paddocks next to stables.

What made this such a brilliant plan of escape was that they were inside the gated community on bicycles, which allowed them to easily travel in any direction. If anyone tried to pursue them in a vehicle, they wouldn't be able to follow them on the narrow horse trails. Likewise, anyone following them on foot wouldn't be able to keep up with them on their bikes. They had obviously calculated that committing a shooting at 6:00 a.m. wouldn't attract much attention since many residents were just waking up. If someone were to call the Sheriff's station to report a shooting, the responding deputies could quickly block off Mt. Olive Drive at the base of the hill. Since this is the only street exit leaving the Thompson house, they could easily be apprehended if they use that route of escape.

Using bicycles to proceed through the gated community was a brilliant escape plan. As the shooters furiously pedaled down the country lane, they heard a gunshot on their right side. They couldn't determine where the shooter was, so they didn't know what to do but to continue down Woodlyn Lane. The gunfire only caused the killers to cycle harder and faster. Their objective was to get out of the area before law enforcement converged on the community. Leaning forward over the bikes, they hoped to make themselves a more difficult target to hit. Ahead, they could see where the road intersected one another. They veered to the left, heading for the southern Woodlyn Lane gate.

The road at that point slightly slopes downward, which allowed them to coast on their bikes, thereby saving their energy. Flying as fast as the bikes could travel, they approached the gate. This particular gate didn't utilize a live guard but had an underground sensor to recognize when someone was waiting to leave. The gate sprang open, allowing the killers to leave the community. They briskly pedaled even harder as they headed for the immediate cross street, which was North Royal Oaks

Drive. Both picked up speed attempting to dart across the road. As they approached the road, they came face to face with a STOP sign. Only a minute before, they had heard someone shooting at them, so they ignored the STOP sign. At this hour in the morning, what was the likelihood that there would be any cross traffic?

What they didn't realize was that Ms. Wilma Johnson was late for work and had to drop off her bloodhound dog at a groomer a short distance away. She wasn't speeding in her van, but her mind was fixed on reaching the groomer's as fast as possible so she wouldn't be late to work. Her focus was on her dog seated next to her in the front passenger seat. She had driven this road many times, so she didn't have to concentrate much on her driving. As she drove toward the South entrance to Bradbury, she didn't need to slow down since she clearly had the right of way. Traffic exiting Bradbury at this blind 'Tee' intersection had to stop.

She had glanced down at her dog, who was napping. Immediately she looked up at the road in front of her. To her surprise, out of the corner of her eye she saw two bicyclists appear from the south gated entrance of Bradbury. Without stopping, they darted in front of her car. Instantly, she hit the brakes as hard as she could, causing her dog to slide off the front seat onto the floor. She turned the steering wheel to the left in an attempt to miss the last cyclist. Glancing in the direction of two men, she noticed both their faces. They appeared to be young black males who had a stressed look on their faces. She noticed the front cyclist made a maneuver around her and zipped over to the side of the road. However, the second man somehow panicked and lost his balance and fell off the bike onto the asphalt. Hurriedly, he righted himself and looked in her direction as he attempted to throw his leg over the frame of the bike. He didn't make any attempt to talk to her but seemed more consumed with fleeing the scene.

Ms. Johnson didn't know what to make of all of this commotion so early in the morning. She felt guilty that her first concern was for her dog that had slid to the floor. She wanted to say something to the two men to make sure they were all right or possibly warn them to be more careful while biking on country roads. But before she could exit her car, she observed that they had taken the bikes through a small hole in the street fencing and had disappeared from view. She pulled her car alongside the hole and looked down into what used to be the streetcar tracks, which now had been made into a regional bike path. By then she couldn't see either of the men who disappeared from the bike path that headed to Pasadena. She helped her dog back into the passenger seat and petted him on the head, then turned her full attention to getting to the groomer's on time.

Her day continued to be busy but uneventful. By 6:00 p.m. she returned to pick up her dog at the groomers when she noticed yellow crime scene tape and several Sheriff's vehicles. This aroused her curiosity, so she pulled over to talk to one of the deputies. She was told that two people had been shot and the suspects had gotten away. A manhunt was underway to find the killers. She asked when this all happened and the deputy said he believed it occurred around 6:00 a.m. Ms. Johnson thought for a moment and reflected on her chance encounter with the two black bicyclists around the same time that morning. She didn't know whether or not to say anything to the deputies. As she was walking away, she hesitated, trying to figure out in her mind what to do. Then she turned toward the deputies and said in an apologetic voice, "This morning I saw two black men riding madly out of the south gate shortly after 6:00 a.m."

The one deputy didn't know if this information was worth kicking up the chain of command or merely a bigoted lady who wanted to blame everything bad on blacks.

To be on the safe side, the deputy asked her for her name and phone number and then indicated he would pass the information on to the detectives. Ms. Johnson had to find another way home since Royal Oaks Drive was still closed off. It wasn't long before she was contacted by the Sheriff's station and asked more specific questions as to what she had seen. The next day, a forensic artist was sent to her place of business to work with her on creating a composite drawing of the two male bicyclists.

Another woman who was driving north on Mt. Olive Drive that morning also saw two black bicyclists wildly riding directly in front of her. She was startled to see them go across the bike path. What caught her attention was that both had backpacks on and the intensity in which they were riding their bikes. When she later learned about the double murders, she mentioned her sighting to the local Sheriff's station. Quickly, the Sheriff sent the same forensic artist to meet with her. She worked with the artist to create another composite drawing of the two cyclists.

(The next graphic page shows the route the bicyclists used to escape. Also, the two composite drawings were based on the descriptions given by two women who claimed they saw the suspects riding bicycles.)

Graphic 4

SHOOTERS' ESCAPE ROUTE
March 16, 1988 6:05 a.m.

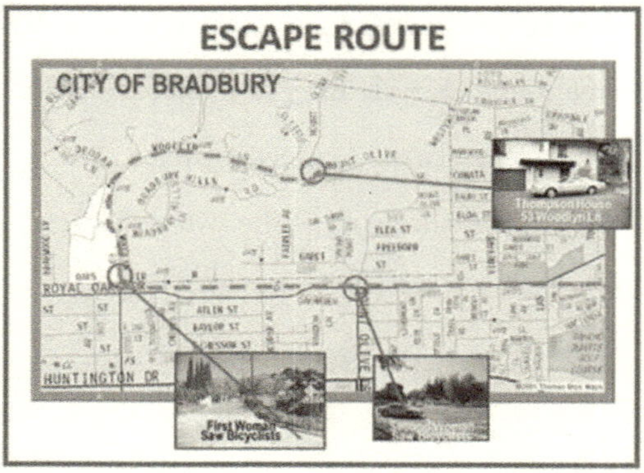

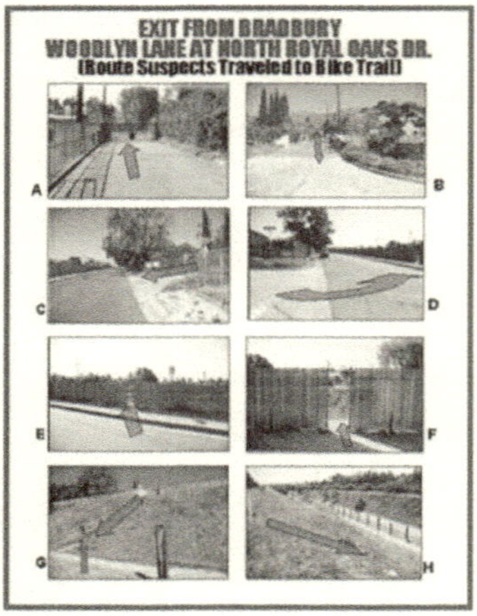

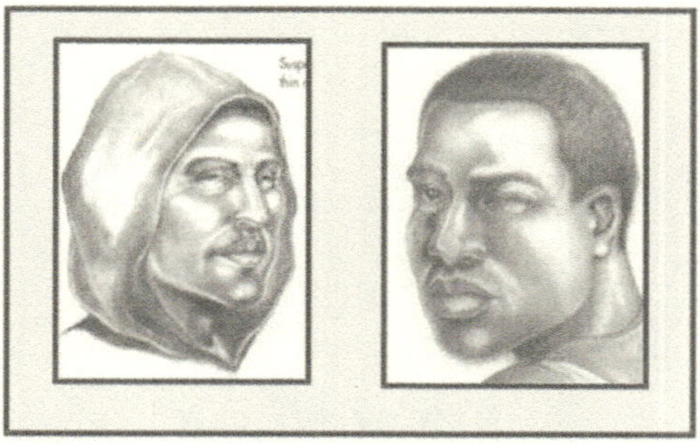

Composite drawings of suspects

CHAPTER 5. WITNESSES TO THE SHOOTING

Fourteen-year-old Allison Triarsi stumbled out of bed realizing it was time to get up if she wanted to be on time for school. She was a typical teenager growing up in Bradbury, living a good life surrounded by horses and all the perks of the well-heeled. The Triarsi's house was directly across from the Thompson's estate, on top of a knoll across a mini valley separated by Woodlyn Lane. Allison and her family were acquainted with Mickey and Trudy. They didn't consider themselves close friends but merely as neighbors who chatted with each other when they were coming or going up their respective driveways.

At 6:05 a.m., Allison was taking a shower when she heard a crackling sound like fireworks or possible gunfire. This startled her since in peaceful Bradbury such loud noises didn't occur. Her mother yelled and told her to get out of the shower and lie on the floor. Children growing up in the ghetto or barrio are programmed when they hear gunfire to immediately run to the bathroom and lie down in the bathtub for their own protection. But, Allison, having grown up in the 'Tranquil City' of Bradbury, had not been well educated in these basic self-preservation techniques.

She grabbed a towel and lay down near their sliding glass door. From that position, she could view the Thompson's driveway, where she could make out the figures of two males. In order to get a better view, she scurried to the living room panoramic window and gazed out in the direction of the noise. At first Allison couldn't be certain where the sound from their voices was coming from. Before she could assess the situation, there was another burst of noise, sounding more like gunfire. Now she could pinpoint the noise as coming from the driveway of the Thompson household. She stood on her tippy toes to get a better view of what was happening. Her entire body was exposed from the outside by the panoramic window. Any gunman looking from the Thompson property could have made an easy target of Allison as she was leaning against the window.

From Allison's vantage point, she could see two men in the Thompson driveway with guns in their hands. Then she heard Trudy Thompson scream something like, "Don't shoot, don't." It was a piercing sound like a frantic call for help. Even though Allison had never heard Trudy scream, she had no doubt this was Trudy's voice, and this was confirmed when she saw Trudy as she appeared to be crawling down the driveway toward the street.

Allison's mind was having difficulty processing what her senses were telling her. It was like watching a movie unfold before her eyes. This couldn't be real. By then Allison's dad, Anthony Triarsi, came into the living room as she looked shocked at her father, wanting an explanation. Was this really happening, or was it a bad nightmare? Then, there was a louder voice, seemingly coming from the top of the driveway. They immediately recognized the voice as Mickey's. "Don't harm my wife," Mickey seemed to be pleading with one of the two attackers. Again, in a booming voice, "Please don't harm my wife." They could see Mickey on the ground looking down the long driveway at Trudy.

What happened next was surreal. The attacker next to Mickey raised his hand in a waving motion that seemed to signal the attacker at the bottom of the driveway, who was by then standing over Trudy. That attacker stood erect and took his hand with the gun and placed it next to Trudy's head. By this time, Trudy's body had curled into the fetal position with her arms stretched upward as though they could protect her from another gunshot.

Without a word being spoken, the attacker standing over Trudy pulled the trigger and Trudy's head jerked downward. In quick succession, he shot a second time to Trudy's skull, causing her head to hit the concrete of the street gutter. As Allison and her father watched from their living room window, they could observe Trudy's body go limp, curling up in a ball, totally lifeless. Allison looked at her dad for a justification to what they both had witnessed. He looked dumbfounded and couldn't find words to describe what they had seen.

Within seconds, their attention was directed to the top of the driveway where they had seen Mickey. They couldn't make out the sounds of agony coming from Mickey. Could it be someone pleading for an answer to a question, "Why, why?" As they saw the attacker at the bottom run up the driveway, they could make out the attacker on top pointing his gun at Mickey, and then they heard more gunfire. By this time, Mickey was lying on the asphalt with his head tilted to the side. His attacker positioned himself next to Mickey's head and, in execution fashion, placed the gun within inches of his head and squeezed the trigger. Almost in slow motion, the shooter repositioned the gun to Mickey's temple and pulled the trigger again.

When was this nightmare going to end? Then there was complete silence. Allison and her dad's adrenaline level had gone off the charts. Their sense of hearing was elevated from all the excitement. Their ears could hear a faint breeze through the eucalyptus trees. Then they cued in on the strange sound of bicycle chains clanking against metal chain guards. They couldn't see the shooters any longer, only the noise of the pedaling of the bikes, which grew fainter and fainter.

Their task at that moment was figuring out how a human being should respond to a double homicide. This was not a common occurrence for them or for most people. Then their instincts kicked in, which was to render aid. Both Allison and her dad ran out their front door and headed down their driveway, which exited onto Woodlyn Lane. Suddenly they heard the sharp sound of more gunfire. The shots seemed to be coming from the area of Dr. Jordan's (pseudonym) house, which was located directly behind the Thompson house. Allison and her dad hesitated for a moment, listening for any more gunfire. Since it had ceased, they continued on their mission to check out Trudy, who was laying in the gutter.

When they reached the street, they had a clear view of Trudy's body curled up in a ball. She was dressed in a western outfit with her cowboy boots on. As they slowly approached, they could see no movement, only a trickle of blood oozing into the gutter. Allison's dad leaned over to check for any signs of life and uttered her name. "Trudy, can you hear me?" There was no response. A puzzled look came over Mr. Triarsi's face as he pondered what to do next.

His only thought was to check on the condition of Mickey, who was at the top of the driveway. Allison stood petrified as to what to do or say. When her father started up the long driveway, she followed in hopes that her dad knew what to do to make everything right. As they reached the top, they looked to their left and could see Mickey's body, dressed all in black with a large pool of blood surrounding his head area. By now his blood was trickling down the driveway. No signs of life could be seen as Mickey lay flat on the asphalt driveway. Mr. Triarsi leaned over to make a cursory check for life, and finding none, he stood up and looked at his daughter and shook his head in disbelief.

(The following graphic page shows the view the Triarsis had of the shooting and where they went to check on Trudy.)

Graphic 5

WITNESSES TO THE SHOOTING

March 16, 1988 6:10 a.m.

VIEW FROM TRIARSI'S HOUSE

(Can See Both Victims' Bodies)

VIEW FROM TRIARSI'S HOUSE

(Looking Down on Crime Scene)

CHAPTER 6. WITNESSES TO THE ESCAPE

Those last shots emanated from Dr. Lance Jordan's house, which was directly behind the Thompson estate. Dr. Jordan and his family had been neighbors of Mickey and Trudy for over ten years. That morning he and his family were still in bed when they heard a series of gunshots that woke them up. Dr. Jordan had been in the military, so he recognized the sound to be that of a 9mm being fired. The gunfire startled him, and he immediately sprung out of bed and dashed to the bedroom window to see if he could determine the origin of the gunshots. He threw open the window and could clearly hear Mickey's voice shouting at the top of his lungs, "Please don't hurt my wife." Mickey continued to scream several more times as his voice crackled with the sound of terror.

Then there was a loud series of shots in rapid succession, which echoed off the hillside. Then a deafening silence filled the air. Dr. Jordan tried to regroup his thoughts. He and Mickey had a close neighborly rapport. He usually talked to Mickey several times a week. Mickey was always working in his auto barn, which was off to the side of the Jordan residence. He remembered that Mickey had called his house the day before when he was not home. Mickey had left a message on Dr. Jordan's answering machine about something that was concerning him. Since Dr. Jordan had returned home late, he had not followed up on Mickey's call. He didn't know what was concerning Mickey, but he had a good idea what it might be.

On prior occasions, Mickey had expressed to him concern about their safety because he had reason to believe his ex-partner might try to kill him. Dr. Jordan had found it hard to believe that anyone would want to harm Mickey. Now, hearing the gunfire originating from Mickey's residence, coupled with the blood-curdling screams from Mickey, Dr. Jordan connected the dots and believed Mickey and Trudy had been attacked.

As a result, Dr. Jordan grabbed his gun from his nightstand, quickly loaded it, and raced over to the front window of the bedroom. Since he was having his house painted, the window screens had been taken off. He stuck his head out of the second-floor window and looked and listened. All he could hear was the clanking of what sounded like bicycle chains hitting a metal guard. He looked in the direction where the noise was coming from and could make out the image of two black males madly riding 10-speed bicycles down the bridle path coming from the rear of the Thompson house. As the bicyclists approached the bottom of the path, they veered slightly to the right and proceeded westbound on Woodlyn Lane, which ran in front of Dr. Jordan's house. His house was set back from the lane by a horse corral. Dr. Jordan could clearly make out that both the bicyclists were two black males with dark clothing and each one wearing a sizable backpack.

Thinking that these people had just shot the Thompsons, he yelled at them to stop. Neither rider seemed to react to his shouts. They didn't even turn their heads in his direction. Believing that these were the shooters who were trying to get away, Dr. Jordan had to make a split-second decision. From what he had heard from the various shots and Mickey's screams, he believed these were murder suspects trying to get away. Dr. Jordan pointed his gun in the bicyclists' direction and shot once in hopes of stopping them. This didn't seem to faze the bicyclists, and they kept on riding, at full speed, down the small country lane and out of view.

At the same time, Dr. Jordan had his wife call the Sheriff's Department to report the incident. The dispatcher related that several Sheriff's cars had been sent to the location. Dr. Jordan, being a long-time resident, knew that the shooters could easily get lost in all the twisty lanes and might be captured within the walled city of Bradbury. He knew that the direction the suspects were going would mean that they would likely try to escape by using the south gate. Dr. Jordan thought that in all likelihood the responding Sheriff's deputies wouldn't use the south entrance. He raced out of his house and jumped into his truck and sped to the south gate hoping to find the suspects stuck inside the locked gate. However, to his disappointment he discovered that the south gate locking system was broken and people could easily go in and out without the need of a key or pass card.

Dr. Jordan didn't know what to do. But everyone has moments when they say, "Why isn't there a cop around when you need one?" Dr. Jordan was in desperate need of a cop, and right before his eyes was a Sheriff's unit pulling into the south gate. He ran over to him waving his hands to get his attention. Since he was slightly out of breath, he yelled that the two black men had gone down Royal Oaks Drive. The deputy had a perplexed look on his face as to what this person was talking about. The deputy indicated he was responding to a crime scene where a shooting occurred, and then he sped up Woodlyn Lane toward the Thompson house. Dr. Jordan felt almost naked, standing all alone at the south gate, realizing the shooters were getting away because he hadn't adequately conveyed to the deputy that he was talking about the shooting the deputy was responding to.

Dr. Jordan kicked himself for not being more assertive with the deputy. All he could think about was getting back in his truck and returning to his house. When he arrived home, he saw deputy sheriff's cars zooming in all directions on Woodlyn Lane below the Thompson house. Dr. Jordan could see Mickey's body lying on the asphalt driveway. His fears were confirmed that Mickey had been killed. A cloud of guilt filled his heart, in that he never returned Mickey's phone call from the night before. Was Mickey trying to warn him? Was Mickey going to ask him to be on the lookout for strangers? Could he have prevented this from happening if only he had been more responsive?

He now felt his duty to Mickey was to convey to the Sheriff's Deputies what he knew about his ex-business partner. He approached one of the responding officers, a Deputy Martinez, and asked if he could talk to him about some of Mickey's concerns. The Deputy stepped to the side and reached for his pen and paper in order to take notes. They stood near Deputy Martinez's police car so the deputy had something to write on. Dr. Jordan tried to organize his thoughts in his mind as he told the deputy that Mickey had had a falling out with his business partner that resulted in a bitter dispute. Their partnership was dissolved, and Mickey had sued his partner for the losses. Just recently, Mickey had finally won the lawsuit between them.

As a result, Dr. Jordan related, Mickey had been threatened by his ex-partner, causing Mickey to be in fear for his life and that of his wife, Trudy. The deputy took notes, realizing this could be crucial information in this double homicide. Dr. Jordan couldn't remember the ex-partner's name, or even where he lived, but he said that he was sure he could find out the information by making several phone calls, which he did. In short order, the Sheriff's Department had a complete description of Mickey's ex-partner, who was a white, middle-aged male who lived in the beach area of Orange County.

Initially, the Sheriff's deputies at the crime scene had two separate descriptions of the suspects. The two women, in their separate cars, claimed the suspects were two black males. This was further supported by Dr. Jordan's description that the two bicyclists were black males. However, Dr. Jordan was asserting that Mickey was in fear of his ex-partner, who was a middle-aged white male. The deputies recognized they had a problem in knowing what type of description to disseminate to the news media. They needed the public's support in solving this case. In order for the public to help, they needed to know the general description and type of person they were looking for.

CHAPTER 7. LOOKING FOR CRIME SCENE EVIDENCE

The call went out to the Sheriff's Homicide Bureau that they were needed to respond to a double homicide in Bradbury. The responding detectives weren't even familiar with the existence of the small town of Bradbury. No one could remember ever having to respond to a homicide in this exclusive township. When the word came in that it involved Mickey Thompson's residence, the lieutenant in charge had additional homicide detectives dispatched to the scene. Upon the arrival of the first Homicide team, they made a cursory view of the two dead bodies on the long driveway. First order of business was to receive a briefing by the patrol sergeant who had collected all the preliminary information from the various deputies who had talked to neighbors and bystanders.

It was confirmed that the body at the top of the driveway was that of Mickey Thompson. The detectives didn't need to ask the question, 'who was Mickey Thompson?' One of the detectives quietly responded, "Oh my God." It wasn't clear whether he meant it as a surprise that a legend had died, or that he realized this was going to be a tough case to solve. When the initial briefing was over, one homicide team was assigned to search the crime scene for physical evidence. Their objective was to find anything that could shed light on how the killings occurred and possibly reveal who committed the murders. These detectives would search for relevant evidence, mark it, see to it being photographed, and ultimately bag it for later forensic testing.

The most obvious physical evidence was the shell casings, which were scattered all over the driveway. The ballistics and firearms identification could be critical in this case, especially if the weapons were ever recovered. Even if the weapons were never recovered, the shell casings can tell how many weapons were used as well as how they were used. They started marking all the various spent shell casings by placing large evidence markers next to each casing. However, what was unusual was that the detectives found at least **four live rounds**. This could indicate that the shooters were trying to threaten the victims by pulling the slide back on their automatic weapons. Or, the shooters were nervously pulling the slides back just to make sure the guns were loaded. They knew that the crime lab would be able to shed some light on the significance of those **live rounds**.

Since there were ejected shell casings, that meant the shooters were using automatics in lieu of revolvers. After examining the shells, the detectives could see that the automatic weapons were 9mm's. Later it was confirmed the spent shells had been fired by two separate guns. This supported what the eyewitnesses had indicated, that there were two shooters. All the shells were photographed where they were found and placed into marked envelopes for transportation back to the crime lab for analysis.

Also found on the driveway were small portions of broken fingernails. The detectives had earlier noticed that Trudy's hands showed signs that her fingernails had been broken off. The fingernails that were found appeared to match Trudy's broken nails. What this indicated was that Trudy most likely was crawling on her hands and knees when she broke her fingernails against the rough surface of the asphalt driveway.

The CSI team's job included recording the layout of the crime scene. The graphics group started taking measurements of the driveway and the exterior of the house. Sketches and notes were taken so that diagrams could be prepared to create exhibits that might be needed for the later court proceedings. What made it particularly difficult was the fact that the Thompson's driveway was circular with two separate gated entrances. However, the Thompsons mainly used the entrance directly below the garage since it was the shortest way to exit the property. Even though they had large iron gates at both entrances, out of convenience they never closed them.

Mickey never wanted to give the impression of being an elitist. He wasn't comfortable living behind a walled-in fortress. Mickey wanted to appear accessible, and he didn't want walls to separate him from the hardworking people who he identified with. Mickey's idea of security was having a family dog. Their dog basically lived outside and was free to roam around the Thompson property, which included approximately two acres. The detectives noticed the dog when they arrived at the crime scene. The dog acted like any other dog in that he would bark at strangers, after which he would go over to them and give them the 'sniff' approval test. Then the dog went about his business of standing guard at the Thompsons' residence on top of the hill. The dog didn't appear aggressive or overly protective of his masters.

The detectives were more interested in the dog than the dog was interested in them. One of the detectives wondered how someone could come on the Thompsons' property without the dog barking, thus alerting Mickey that someone was outside.

There was no question that the dog's bark was a deep husky woof that could be heard from the other end of the property. Another detective involved in collecting the physical evidence mentioned that he had discovered a Taser, better known as a stun gun, lying on the side of the driveway halfway down. The one detective pondered the relationship between a dog barking and the Taser. Could the Taser have been used to stun the dog and keep it from barking?

It was strange to find a Taser device at a crime scene. A Taser is used to incapacitate a person or animal by a high-voltage shock. They aren't used very often by law enforcement since it requires the user to be in close contact with the person in order to shock them. Most police officers don't want to be that close to a violent suspect with only a stun gun in their hand.

The detectives examined the stun gun and found the bottom cover had been removed and something like duct tape was used to hold the battery in place. Possibly the cover had been lost or purposely removed, in order to prevent it from being identifiable from its serial number. Without the cover there was no way to trace the stun gun back to its owner.

The stun gun perplexed the detective since they couldn't decipher why it was on the side of the driveway. It was found in the area where some of the shell casings were found. It was logical to assume that one of the attackers had brought it and had somehow dropped it. Later the crime lab checked it for latent prints, but none were found. Then the detectives wondered why the attackers would have brought it in the first place. What were its purpose and use?

One possibility was that it was used to stun Mickey so he would be incapacitated and would be alive to watch the attackers kill Trudy in front of him. However, the autopsy didn't reveal any part of Mickey's body that had suffered a Taser burn, nor was there any indication from Mickey's clothes that a Taser had been used.

The big question was how the attackers could have taken Mickey by surprise and so suddenly debilitate him. Mickey was in good physical health, and being a former Marine he would have been able to take on anyone who tried to attack him. How could the attackers have confronted Mickey without being attacked by him? Somehow, the attackers had to take him by surprise. The easiest way was for the attackers to wait in the bushes across from the garage. When Mickey emerged from the back of the garage, he would pass by the person only several feet away. At that point, they could jump out with the stun gun and try to shock him. This approach would certainly have caught Mickey by surprise.

Since there was no evidence the stun gun had been used on Mickey, possibly the attackers at the last minute had abandoned the idea of using it. When they saw Mickey turn the corner of the garage, they may have been surprised by his size and decided not to have any physical contact with him. What is known as a fact is that the garage door had three bullet holes in it. That meant that the shooter was standing in or near the shrubbery when he fired his gun. If he fired at Mickey when he turned the corner of the garage, the trajectory of the bullets fired from the bushy area would mean the slugs would strike the garage door exactly where the bullet holes were found.

Everything at that point was mere speculation as to where the shooters had been located. When Mickey walked out of the garage, he passed by the orange tree. One of the CSI technicians noticed that there were orange peelings on the ground in the bushy area next to the driveway. These orange peels indicated that someone had peeled an orange shortly before the shooting. At 6:00 a.m. it was unlikely that anyone, other than the attackers, had peeled the orange. This evidence also indicated the shooters had been waiting for the Thompsons. This could later be used to prove the special allegation of Lying-in-Wait. In other words, the shooters had plenty of time while they waited, as evidenced by the orange peelings.

(The following graphic page shows where the various items of evidence were found in the driveway.)

Graphic 6

EVIDENCE AT CRIME SCENE

X is where suspects were hiding.

Some of the shots struck garage door.

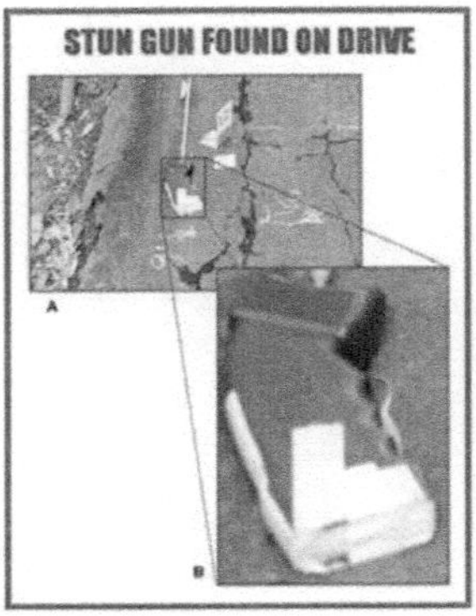

Stun gun was on driveway

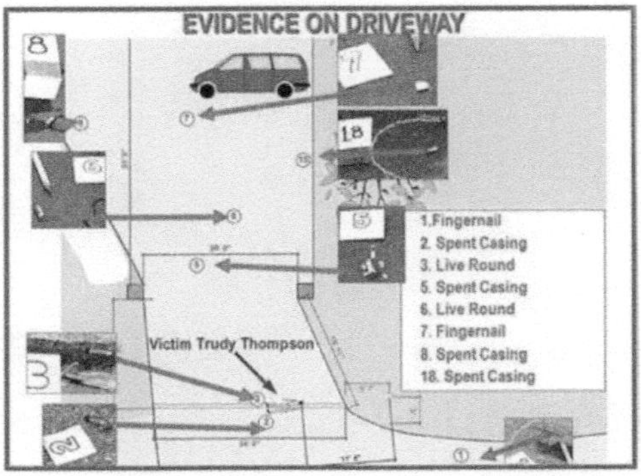

Where various items were found on driveway

CHAPTER 8. INVESTIGATION OF THE EX-PARTNER

Since the entire driveway was considered a giant crime scene, the various detectives and the CSI crew were examining every square inch of the Thompson property. They noticed a Lincoln Continental parked directly in front of the house. It was considered one of the most stylish and trendy cars of its time, and the Thompsons used it for more formal occasions. It had a personalized license plate of 'MT TT' for both Mickey and Trudy Thompson, which exemplified the close bond they had for each other. Anyone who knew them recognized that they were an inseparable pair. When the detectives checked out the Lincoln, they found that it hadn't been used that morning since the engine was cold and the doors were locked.

The Toyota minivan appeared to be the vehicle that had been used since it had the keys in it and the engine was still warm. After calling Mickey's business in Anaheim, the detectives learned that Mickey and Trudy drove the minivan the 30 miles daily to their office in Anaheim. It wasn't the type of vehicle one would expect the fastest man on earth to drive. One expected to see Mickey in a classy sports car. However, Mickey had a practical side when it came to business. At this stage in his life, he didn't have to impress anyone by driving a flashy, extravagant car.

The detectives were trying to determine how the minivan came to rest against a small retaining wall a third of the way down the driveway. Either Trudy had backed the minivan into this position, or it had rolled back to where the rear of the vehicle collided against a block retaining wall.

When the detectives examined the minivan, they found several bullet holes through the front windshield and driver's side door window. Since there was broken glass below the driver's window, it appeared that the attacker had shot at the minivan where the vehicle had come to rest. Possibly Trudy was inside the minivan when it was fired at.

The passenger door window had been shattered by a bullet that had become lodged in the inside of the door. When the detectives examined the inside of the minivan, they looked inside the center console, between the front seats. There they found a cloth bag about the size of a fist that was full of expensive jewelry. This surprised the detectives, who didn't know what to make of that fact. After the detectives talked to close friends, they learned that Trudy always kept a set of her daily jewelry in the console. They said that she would decide what she wanted to wear, take those pieces out, and leave the rest of her jewelry tucked in the bag in the console. In other words, Trudy didn't want to waste time at home trying to figure out what jewelry she should wear at work.

When Trudy's body was examined, she had on several pieces of expensive gold jewelry. All this made it appear that **the shooters were not robbers**. The jewelry she was wearing and what was found in the console was valued at over $20,000. Since the shooters didn't take any of the jewelry or any of the cash Mickey had on him, the detectives discounted robbery as the motive for the attack.

Since robbery wasn't the motive for the shooting, the detectives began to focus on the information the detectives had received from Dr. Jordan and others that it possibly was a retaliation attack on Mickey by his former business partner. The detectives at the house huddled together and it was agreed that two detectives should locate the ex-business partner, Michael Goodwin, and find out if he had anything to do with the attack. Sgt. Ray Verdugo was one of the detectives assigned to track down Goodwin.

Sgt. Verdugo had Goodwin's name run through the various computer systems. That was when he learned that the business partner lived in Orange County. They came up with a phone number and directly contacted him. Goodwin indicated that he would be happy to talk to them at his attorney's office. Sgt. Verdugo thought that was a strange request but went along with it. Two detectives, without delay, traveled to the attorney's office in Huntington Beach. When they arrived, they announced to the receptionist that they were there to meet with Mr. Michael Goodwin. The receptionist made a phone call and then turned to the detectives and instructed them to wait in the lobby. They complied and waited. They had never met or seen a photo of Goodwin. Later while they were waiting in the lobby, they noticed a middle-aged man rush past the receptionist and enter the attorney's office. After a short wait, the attorney came out and invited the detectives in and inquired as to what they wanted. They said that they wanted to talk to Michael Goodwin about a homicide case they were investigating.

The attorney indicated that he needed more information about the homicide before he could advise Mr. Goodwin whether or not to speak to them. By this time, the detectives realized that the middle-age man with the red hair standing behind the attorney was in fact, Michael Goodwin. Everyone sat down in the attorney's office, but Goodwin continued to stand. The attorney explained that his client, Mr. Goodwin, had been in a heated lawsuit with Mickey Thompson. He related the lawsuits had gone all the way to the U.S. Supreme Court. The attorney said he didn't want Mr. Goodwin to answer any questions since litigation was still pending. He indicated Mr. Goodwin was in fear of his life and the same people who had killed Mickey Thompson were also out to get him.

The detectives said they weren't interested in the civil lawsuit but only wanted to talk to Mr. Goodwin about his activities during the morning hours of March 16, 1988. What was interesting was that Goodwin stood behind his attorney not saying a word but made a jester with his lips as though they were sealed because of his attorney's advice. This wasn't the reception Detective Verdugo had expected. What could they infer from the fact that the prime suspect wouldn't make himself available for questioning?

Goodwin's attorney, in his most accommodating voice, stated that Mr. Goodwin wanted to fully cooperate with the investigation but was in deadly fear for his own safety. The detectives knew they didn't have sufficient probable cause to arrest Michael Goodwin for the murders of Mickey and Trudy Thompson. All they had was Dr. Jordan's hearsay statement that Mickey had told him that he was concerned for his safety, and that if anything happened to him authorities should check out his former business partner. The detectives walked out of the attorney's office realizing this wasn't going to be a case solved in a couple of days. Now they knew they were going to have to build a case from the ground up, without the help of Goodwin or obtaining any statements from him.

(These are photos of the minivan and the layout of the Thompson Estate)

Graphic 7

CRIME SCENE

March 16, 1988 6:05 a.m.

This is Minivan Trudy was driving Trudy's jewelry still in van

Diagram showing the two driveway entrances and the placement of the vehicles

CHAPTER 9. Who Are the Suspects?

The detectives had an assessment conference to decide in what direction they should concentrate their efforts. The news media had reported to the public that witnesses had seen two black males riding away on bicycles. This information had been released by the Sheriff's Department in order to obtain the public's cooperation in looking for the killers. Unfortunately, some people in the media spun the facts of the Mickey Thompson Murders into a racial issue by saying, "*The Thompsons were gunned down in the driveway of their palatial estate in the gated community of Bradbury by two black males.*" The public tried to digest this startling information. In many people's minds, what was to be made of the fact that Mickey and his wife were white and they lived in an exclusive white neighborhood? The adjacent communities had a sizeable black population, many of whom could be described as poor. Could this be a case of Robin Hood stealing from the rich to give to the poor? Or, could this be some type of race war in which some poor blacks were striking back at wealthy whites who lived above them in a gated community? Was Mickey Thompson selected because he was rich and well known or most of all because he was white?

The Sheriff's Department had to be careful not to create racial fears in the minds of the white folks living in the San Gabriel Valley. The public can accept the fact there are murderers in their community. Everyone understands that there will always be robberies or disputes that result in people being killed. Gang violence and domestic violence continually occurs and seems to be part of the price one pays for living in an urban society. The public recognizes that such violence does happen. In order to survive this environment, one learns how to protect one's self from being a victim. People can prevent being a victim of a robbery by not wearing expensive jewelry in public, which is a 'No Brainer.' Or, one learns to stay out of gang territory by changing one's driving habits to steer around known gang territory. However, when one fears being attacked by another race, there is a paranoid tendency created to avoid people of that race. As irrational as this may be, in fact, it can become a real fear.

As the news of a double murder spread, there was guarded concern about the safety of people who were white and affluent. To some this could have been the beginning of a race war. The homicide detectives had become all too familiar with the race war concept. Many of these same detectives were around during the Manson Family murders, in which Charles Manson was trying to create a race war. In order to create racial violence, Manson had his followers brutally attack whites and steal their credit cards. Then he took the victim's credit cards and planted them in black communities where they would be found by blacks. The idea was that the blacks would use the credit cards and then get caught. Then the police would assume the blacks had committed the murders of the whites. His concept of 'Helter Skelter' was that the whites would believe that the blacks were after them and there would be a giant war between the races. Manson's scheme had him hiding out until the war was over and the blacks would ask him to rule the country because they wouldn't be able to do it themselves. As bizarre as this concept may seem, it really happened. The detectives didn't want to provide any fuel to starting another race war.

Specifically, whites in the community breathed a sigh of relief when the media started providing more details about the business dispute between Mickey and

Goodwin. At that point, people rationalized the murders as a falling out between business partners that had nothing to do with racial retaliation against the rich and famous whites.

The Sheriff's detectives expanded their investigation into the possibility that it was Mickey's old business partner who had ordered a hit on the Thompsons. It wasn't long before the detectives were inundated with all sorts of information about bad blood between the two. It seemed that Goodwin had a strong motive to hate Mickey. Was there evidence that Goodwin actually had something to do with the Thompsons' murders?

(The following graphic page shows a Relationship of Parties chart)

Graphic 8

PARTIES INVOVED IN CASE

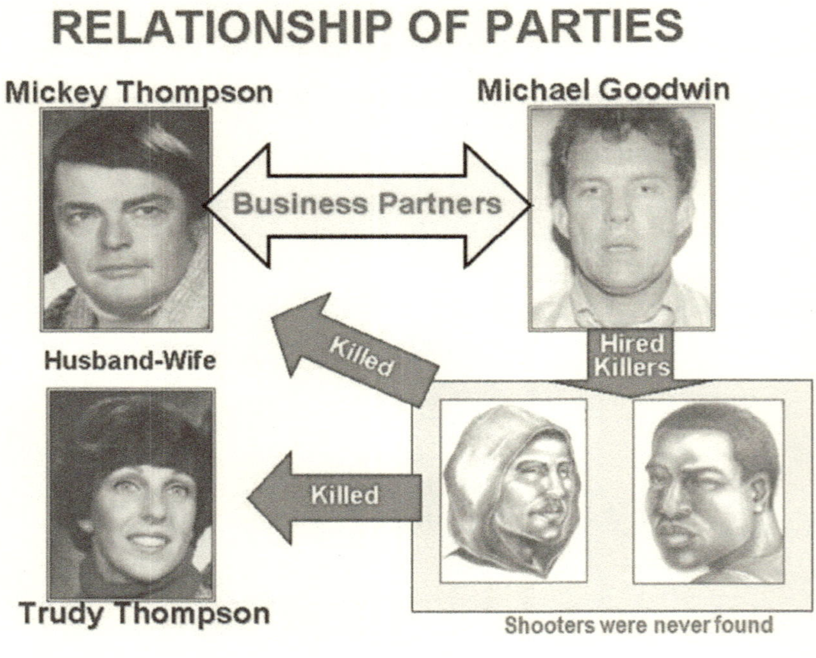

CHAPTER 10. WHO WAS MICKEY THOMPSON?

To understand Mickey Thompson as a person, one has to go back to his roots. He and his sister, Colleen, grew up in the small bedroom community of Alhambra, which borders on the east side of the gigantic metropolis of Los Angeles. It was a fine place for families to live in the 1940s. Mickey's dad was an officer on the Alhambra Police Department and eventually worked his way up to head of the detective bureau. Being the son of the top sleuth in town meant that Mickey had to stay out of trouble, or at least make sure he didn't get caught. Coming from such a tight-knit family, he learned to work hard and try to excel to be the best at whatever he did.

When he was seven years old, he was curious as to how to make a racing car, so he dismantled an old washing machine to create a go-cart, which actually worked. As a teenager, Mickey liked to tinker on old clunkers and relished the challenge to make them run. Once he had accomplished that, his next task was to see how fast he could make them go. Those were the days when cars didn't have computers, and anyone with a socket set and a torque wrench could rebuild an engine. To make a car go faster either required the boring out the cylinders in the engine block or shaving the heads. Every adolescent male knew this would increase the compression ratio, thereby resulting in more power.

Male juveniles would save up their money to buy a 'racing cam,' which would guarantee an added 20 horsepower. That was back when life was simpler, without fuel injection, and any kid could adjust a carburetor with a screwdriver. A status symbol for a young male was installing a four-barrel Stromberg carburetor. This was the equivalent to squirting a gasoline hose into the cylinders. It increases the power in the converse ratio of the miles per gallon. The end result was a high-powered gas guzzler.

For Mickey, souping up old jalopies wasn't a mere hobby but a passion to build the best and the fastest. Every time he worked on a car, he learned something new. But Mickey was different from the average teenage mechanic because he would analyze what he was doing and make mental notes to himself as to how he could enhance the engine's performance in the future. With every improvement he had to test it out to see if in fact it worked. If not, then it was back to the drawing board until he figured it out.

After high school, he felt he had to move on with his life and realized he didn't excel at academics so he turned to the armed services. Mickey always wanted to be the very best at whatever he did, so it was a natural fit for him to join the U. S. Marine Corps. This may have been one of the smartest decisions Mickey ever made. With the corps motto of 'Semper Fidelis' (always faithful), the Marines provided him with the discipline he needed and the dogged determination, both of which assisted him later in life to be successful.

In the early 1950s, dragster racing became popular partly because any young man with a car and a spark plug gap gauge could participate. With four wheels and a large-block engine, the sky was the limit. Muscle cars were the rage, and slight modifications could make any street-legal car a roaring machine. The spectators filled the stands of the drag strips to watch 'egos race' to see who had the fastest car. Quarter mile racing strips popped up wherever there was a straight road of asphalt on the outskirts of town. The roar of the engines was deafening, and the smell of burning tire rubber filled the air. Male testosterone levels reached record heights.

As the sport of drag racing grew, the street legal cars had to yield to monster machines whose only purpose was to go from the starting line to the finish line in the shortest amount of time. This was where Mickey's ability to innovate came into play. He realized the importance of tires. The guy who had tires that could grip the track would be flagged the winner. The size of the tires, the tread of the tires, and the pressure of the tires all played a role in how much traction the dragster would have at the starting gates.

Where Mickey became the great innovator was in the design of the dragster. As most builders of dragsters were placing the driver up front or in the middle of the racecar, Mickey designed a completely different dragster. His design placed the driver at the far rear of the dragster, even behind the rear axle in order to improve traction. This concept was called the 'slingshot' dragster, which changed the sport in 1954. Mickey's design propelled the sport of drag racing to hit new speed records.

(The following graphic page provides a review of who Mickey was and what he did.)

Graphic 9

CHAPTER 11. BREAKING RECORDS

The dragster world hooked Mickey on speed, but it was limited to how fast a vehicle could be propelled down a short ¼-mile track. Mickey didn't want to be limited by such a short distance. He was looking at the big picture, which was, how fast could a person travel on land? The early '60s saw significant advances in traveling at high speeds with the use of jet engines and rocket propulsion. Some people were experimenting with racing vehicles on wheels propelled by turbine engines; in essence, flying on land. Mickey wasn't interested in that since his field of expertise was high-performance piston-driven engines. His challenge was to see how fast man could travel in a racecar with conventional engines, utilizing piston power.

In order to try to set a land speed record, Mickey had to further refine all he had learned from his experience with racing dragsters. He now had to consider more than mere high-performance engines; he also had to factor in engine endurance. The aerodynamic design became crucial to cut down on wind resistance. Mickey designed, from scratch, a racecar called the streamliner. The power came from **four** 415 cu. inch Supercharged Pontiac engines coupled to **four** 1937 Cadillac transmissions connected to a four-wheel-drive power train, altogether generating 2800 horsepower. It had to be highly aerodynamic in order to reach such high speeds. He was personally involved every step of the way, from the trial-and-error phase of building the various parts, testing, and modifying the garage-built streamliner named 'Challenger 1.'

On September 9, 1960, at the Bonneville Salt Flats in Utah, Mickey believed the weather conditions were ideal, so he and his crew rolled the Challenger 1 out of the pit area. Mickey was sandwiched into the driver's seat. The car was designed for speed and not for the driver's comfort. Mickey was tightly strapped into the cockpit and focused on breaking the all-time speed record. He didn't dwell on the danger of traveling hundreds of miles per hour. All the safety features now required for such testing, hadn't been invented yet. In those early years, people like Mickey were thought of as daredevils performing a stunt.

As Mickey moved up to the starting point, his adrenaline was racing through his veins. The noise from the engine drowned out any fear he might have had. This was a different challenge for Mickey, in that it wasn't how fast he started and how much distance he covered in five seconds but how long he could continue in a straight line between the timing blocks. Any deviation could reduce the speed and also cause the racecar to lose control and possibly roll over, disintegrating into pieces. This demonstration of speed on the Bonneville Salt Flats was going to test Mickey's ability to steer the vehicle as well as continue to increase the speed. He had devised a unique way of controlling such power by using two accelerators. The trick was knowing how much acceleration to give to each set of engines.

The moment of truth had come for Mickey. Could he live up to the name of the racecar, 'Challenger 1'? Mickey was about to take on the biggest challenge that could change his life forever. The vehicle catapulted forward as he pressed his foot on the accelerators and he could feel the vehicle shake as he pressed even harder on both the accelerators. His dual-accelerators concept required him to distribute the power evenly. Too much on one pedal could cause a disastrous turn to one side. As he rocketed down the track, the noise of the engine was drowned out by the wind racing by the windshield. Since there wasn't anything along the side of the track, he couldn't tell how fast he was traveling, except everything looked like a blur. The racecar was vibrating, and Mickey was struggling to maintain a straight line because of a slight side wind. As he passed the second timer, he pulled his foot off the dual accelerators and wondered if he had reached a speed over 400 mph.

In order to qualify for the world record, Mickey had to maneuver the Challenger 1 around and race back to the starting blocks. His speed would be determined by combining his top speed going in both directions. This rule was created so a racer couldn't use heavy tailwinds to increase the vehicle's speed. By using the speed in both directions, this eliminated anyone receiving an advantage from wind conditions. Mickey had been clocked at 406.60 mph, which would set the world record if he could do the return pass at a similar speed. As Mickey started his return, he stepped hard on the accelerator and the 'Challenger 1' took off like a bullet. His mind flashed the realization that within minutes he would be the world's champion for driving faster than any other person. Everything was perfect until he heard a loud thud then clanking sound as the 'Challenger 1' jerked to one side. As the engines roared, the streamliner's speed came to a crawl. Soon Mickey would learn he had broken an axle and one of the Pontiac engines had blown up, so the claim of making a world record had evaporated into thin air.

Even though he didn't set the **world's speed record**, he did set a land speed record that made him go down in history as the fastest man on earth at that time. Everyone was astonished and impressed by Mickey's accomplishment. Mickey became a folk hero to all the young people who dreamed of breaking some type of speed record. Mickey personified the hero image by being a big guy who had been trained as a Marine and was totally fearless. Later, the Challenger 1 was retired to the National Hot Rod Association Museum in Pomona, California.

Mickey had accomplished part of his dream at least as to becoming the fastest American on wheels, and now it was time to move on to the next great challenge. He had always been intrigued by the Indianapolis 500 race on Memorial Day weekend. Yet this had been a special league of old-timers who built their cars in the traditional method with Offenhauser-powered engines placed in the front of the racecar. Mickey realized he could increase the speed by placing a V-8 Buick engine in the rear of a racecar. In 1962, he had one of his newly designed cars race in the Indy 500. It did well, but it had mechanical problems that prevented it from making it to the winner's circle. However, that year Mickey and his team won the Mechanical Achievement Award for original design, construction, and accomplishment.

He gave it another try in 1963, with a series of five cars of varying designs. He had worked with other builders to create the Harvey Aluminum Special, called the 'Roller Skate' car, which was super lightweight and utilized wider tires. This new design irritated the old-timers, and new rules were created to prevent it from being used in the future.

Mickey didn't waste his time with the Indianapolis 500 races anymore and moved on to other types of racing. To show his versatility, he entered the field of

Funny Cars in the late 1960s. He redesigned the engines and bodies of the Funny Cars, and eventually his car won the National Hot Rod Association (NHRA) racing event.

Mickey raced everything from stock cars to off-road vehicles and continued to engineer various types of competition engines. He returned to Bonneville Salt Flats to try again to obtain the elusive world title. However, each time he either had mechanical or weather problems that plagued him. Eventually, his sponsors lost interest and Mickey re-focused on other forms of racing. As his career veered in various directions, he truly became the quintessential California hot rod driver who won over 500 race titles for speed and endurance, more than any other auto racer. He was an American Racing Legend from the Bonneville Salt Flats to the Indy's brickyard.

(The following graphic page shows Mickey Thompson's Challenger 1 racing at Bonneville Salt Flats, where he went 406 mph.)

Graphic 10

CHALLENGER 1
1960

Racing at Bonneville

Mickey squeezed into challenger1

Mickey went 406.6 mph

The Challenger was powered by four 415 cu. inch Supercharged Pontiac engines connected to four 1937 Cadillac transmission producing 2800 horsepower

CHAPTER 12. BUSINESS VENTURES

Long before his murder, Mickey Thompson was a household name among most people not because of his racing accomplishments but for his business ventures. By the late 1960s, people were asking Mickey to make parts for their vehicles. It started with racing people who recognized Mickey was a genius when it came to designing high-performance auto parts. Then the requests came from his fans who wanted to be able to duplicate his record-breaking exploits. Mickey realized that his success could pay off in large dividends if he made available, for sale, all sorts of engine parts: engine heads, manifolds, cams, or any part that would make a vehicle go faster.

So, by the late 1960s, Mickey Thompson High-Performance Racing Parts became a lucrative business for him. He then expanded his business to include tires. By 1963, the Mickey Thompson Performance tires became a best seller for tough truck tires. The beefy mud and snow tires became as popular as his slick racing tires. To this day, the tire line is still popular.

With all the time Mickey spent at the auto races, he learned what he enjoyed and what other spectators wanted in regards to auto racing events. His appearances at the Indianapolis 500 gave him insight as to what made racing such an exciting sport. The Memorial Day 500 Indianapolis race would draw attendance in the several-hundred-thousand range. This was a once-a-year event held in one venue. Mickey realized that there were thousands of people throughout the country who would be willing to attend auto-racing events if they could enjoy the conveniences they experienced at athletic sporting events such as baseball and football.

Traditionally, racetracks were laid out like the Indianapolis 500, with a large oval track that may cover over a mile. Spectators complained that seating in bleachers provided them with a very limited view of a race that is run around a large, elliptical track. Mickey's idea was to use a **sports stadium** with its wraparound seating. No longer would spectators be restricted to seeing only a small portion of a race, since the race track was directly below them. In this way, they were a part of all the action and this made for a much more exciting spectator sport.

Mickey started by convincing local sports stadiums to conduct races in their facility. In order to convert the stadiums into racetracks, Mickey had to find a way to make thrilling races that would be safe for the spectators and yet not damage the facility. Mickey came up with his own solution, which was to create racing barriers made out of plastic. These barricades could be easily moved around to form a racetrack. Once the barriers were in place, they were filled with water, which made them rigid. These were called the MT (Mickey Thompson) Hydro Barricades. Mickey's concept revolutionized car racing in stadiums.

In order to protect the stadium's grassy infield, he agreed to cover it with tons of dirt. Within hours, Mickey's crews could fill a stadium with so much dirt that the grass was hidden under several feet of soil. The advantage of using all this dirt meant that the track could contain a "twisty turny" racetrack, which made for exhilarating racing. This became Mickey's signature sporting event. He had a team that would go from city to city promoting the event and another crew whose job was set up the racetrack just before race day and then remove all the dirt upon completion of the racing event.

The business started slow but continued to grow as the popularity of stadium racing continued to mature. It wasn't long before the public couldn't get enough of these events. For several years, Mickey's business was flying high. However, over time the expectation from the fans was that they wanted something bigger and better than the previous event. Mickey Thompson events involved racing any type of vehicle, including stock cars, trucks, dragsters, and off-road vehicles. He didn't get involved in motorcycle racing, which had been already carved out by other promoters. Shortly, Mickey felt the agony of success, and he was learning that these events were capable of making a lot of money, but they were also susceptible to losing a huge amount if one wasn't careful.

He was the greatest promoter and the ultimate dealmaker. His name and reputation attracted thousands of spectators. At this stage of his career, he was widely compared to Buffalo Bill, whose real name was William Frederick Cody, and who started out as a soldier, army scout, buffalo hunter, Pony Express rider, fur trapper, gold prospector, and ultimately a showman in the late 1900s. He created the Buffalo Bill Wild West shows, which showcased bronco riding and handling bovine and equine livestock roping. Cody included in his various shows other famous westerners such as Wild Bill Hickok, Annie Oakley, Calamity Jane, and even Sitting Bull. By the turn of the century, the Wild West show traveled all over the country and for many years was a big hit in England and Europe. The success of the show was a direct result of William Cody understanding how to package a show in a way that was convenient and exciting, giving the spectators everything they liked. The main ingredient to Cody's success was his ability to know how to promote it.

Mickey seemed to follow in William Cody's footsteps in knowing how to promote events. Mickey had learned how to pack the stadiums, but his big challenge was making them profitable ventures. This required a detailed person who organized the racers and vendors and worked closely with the stadium. Mickey could hold press conferences and do the promotional pre-events, but when it came to the detail work, he was completely lost.

CHAPTER 13. MEETING TRUDY

With all of Mickey's expertise in business, he couldn't grasp what to do and when to do it. The day-to-day operation bored him, and he didn't have the patience to deal with scheduling, payroll, contracts, and all the meticulous work that occurs behind the scenes. He needed someone he could delegate the mundane tasks to, but it had to be someone he could trust. At that time, Trudy entered into Mickey's life. Her personal traits were the opposite of Mickey's, in that she was a planner and a 'detail person.' Trudy was a perfect match for Mickey. This hardheaded ex-Marine wasn't afraid to race anyone at any time; however, he was afraid to make ordinary business decisions. Trudy stepped up to the plate, having the temperament and organizational skills to run the largest racing events of all times.

Mickey soon realized that Trudy was the essential person to make things work. The two of them truly were a 'dynamic duo.' No one was a better promoter than Mickey, and Trudy was most assuredly the best at being a business manager. They complemented each other in the manner of the way they worked. Mickey concentrated on the big picture, and Trudy quietly worked behind the scenes to make sure everything happened on time. He relied on her greatly to do the things he wasn't capable of doing. They worked as a team and could pull off the biggest sports events and make it look easy. Their success was the envy of everyone who was in the sports entertainment business. Between the two of them, they created the MTEG (Mickey Thompson Entertainment Group), which raked in millions of dollars from dozens of stadium racing events.

Mickey often reflected on the happenstance of how they met. Trudy was working as a secretary at Hot Rod Magazine. Mickey had various contacts with the magazine, and one day he met Trudy while she was working there. Although there was 18 years between their ages, Mickey came across as the confident character who had control of everything around him. Even though Trudy couldn't help but notice Mickey, she recognized that he moved in celebrity circles far above her secretarial pay grade.

Colleen Campbell, Mickey's sister, had seen numerous gold diggers circling like vultures around Mickey waiting for their opportunity to put their sharp talons into his fortune. Colleen had met Trudy, liked her and thought she would be a good match for Mickey, who had suffered through a painful divorce. Trudy came across as a hard worker who wasn't out to impress anyone. Colleen set Trudy up on a date with Mickey. With their diverse personalities, they didn't seem to have much in common. But they both possessed a strong work ethic and believed in keeping their word, and most of all, they enjoyed each other's company.

Their age difference didn't seem to affect their relationship. Needless to say, Mickey liked having a lively lady in his life. It made him feel more virile, and her new perspective helped Mickey better understand the younger generation who patronized his events. For Trudy, it gave her the opportunity to see what it was like to live and move with the rich and famous. She enjoyed the excitement that filled every day with traveling to new venues for more racing events. Being on the arm of Mickey opened doors she would never have been able to enter. Mickey moved in the circle of superstars, sports figures, and politicians, and now Trudy was a part of that life.

It seemed to be a perfect match between two completely different people. Her admiration for him was immeasurable. Mickey could see Trudy as a person who was totally different from himself. She had a softer, gentler approach that served her well when dealing with all types of people. With her prior work experience, she knew everything about the racing business. It was only a matter of time before they both realized that they had a special bond between them.

While they were dating, Mickey recognized Trudy's knowledge and understanding of the business made her a vital asset to his company. As much as Mickey enjoyed their personal life, he also came to the realization that he couldn't lose Trudy's business insight. Mickey's life was so much easier with Trudy being in it. He could concentrate his attention on the promotional side and didn't have to personally become embroiled with the minutiae of the everyday operation. The idea of marriage between the two of them was both a personal decision and maybe a tad more a business decision.

The marriage brought happiness to both of them, and they eventually bought a new house in Bradbury that Trudy made into a delightful home. At this time in Mickey's life, he had accomplished everything in the racing business. He had been a winner in dragster racing, speed record holder at Bonneville Salt Flats, an innovator at the Indy 500, a tough competitor in the Mexican Off Road racing, and an all-time favorite with the Funny Car drag racing competition.

Mickey Thompson's legend was bigger than life. As a result of his many successes, he wasn't someone who was overly modest about his accomplishments. It would be a fair statement to say Mickey had a gigantic ego, which had been earned the hard way. It also would be correct to say that Mickey thought of himself as a perpetual winner, and losing wasn't an option.

Later, Mickey competed in a boat race in which he crashed and was seriously injured. His doctors said he would be paralyzed from the waist down and definitely would never walk again. This was earthshaking for Mickey. He had always been active and didn't want to sit in a wheelchair for the rest of his life. With Trudy's help, he did the physical therapy, and she eventually nursed him back to good health. Mickey was indebted to Trudy for the love and care she showed in her relentless efforts to help him recover. This rehabilitation tested their resolve and proved that as a couple they could take on anything. Eventually, Mickey came back stronger than ever, and their personal and professional lives couldn't have been better. The business was still hugely successful, even though it was very demanding and exhausting.

Sometime in 1982, Trudy began having some health problems. It was unclear whether the health complications were caused by the demands of the business or something else. Mickey loved his wife and didn't want her health to suffer. It most likely was the stress of the job, juggling all the appointments and commitments she had to oversee. Mickey felt guilty that he may have given Trudy too much responsibility in running so many events in one year. It was great for making money, but it wasn't worth jeopardizing Trudy's health.

He began to think of ways he could scale back the business. This wasn't easy to find a way to cut back. So much of the business centered around Mickey as a celebrity. The public expected a "Mickey Thompson Race Event" to involve Mickey Thompson. Mickey started searching for a way to sell off his business and at the same time capitalize on the value of his good name. Who had the experience to run such large stadium races and understand all that was involved in promoting events? The one name that came up as a possible partner for such a merger was Michael Goodwin.

(The following graphic page shows Mickey and Trudy Thompson and their Bradbury home.)

Graphic 11

MICKEY &TRUDY THOMPSON

First met

They dated

Married

Moved to Bradbury & lived on top of hill

Ranch style Home

Stables made into 10 car Garage

CHAPTER 14. MICHAEL GOODWIN THE PROMOTER

In the 1980s, there were other promoters who envied Mickey's business achievements. One of those promoters was Michael Goodwin, who was competing for the same sports fans as Mickey. They appeared to be competitive sports rivals. Goodwin was a brash showman but on a smaller scale than Mickey. Goodwin's initiation into show business began back in the '60s when he promoted the careers of the "Carpenters," a brother-sister musical duo. Karen Carpenter, with her brother Richard, made famous songs like 'Close To You' and 'We've Only Just Begun.' To most people, Christmas wouldn't be complete without hearing Karen's melodic 'Merry Christmas Darling.' Another of Goodwin's credits was his promoting the last stage tour of the psychedelic rock singer and songwriter Janis Joplin. During those years, Goodwin learned that the first tenet of promoting was to generate an incredible amount of publicity for a future event. Basically, it meant it took a cornucopia of money to make a pot full of money. He knew that one had to be willing to take considerable risks if one was to be successful.

Goodwin's childhood was similar to Mickey's in that they both grew up in Southern California. Goodwin's roots were in the Long Beach area, where his father was a Navy man. Young Michael had a nautical background surrounded by the big ships in the harbor. His childhood dream was to be an Admiral in the Navy. As impressed as he was with the big ships, his teenage years were consumed racing around on the fastest motorcycles he could get his hands on. Over the years, he combined his interest in motorcycles with his talent in event planning. He experimented and found a better way to hold motorcycle races by placing them in a stadium type facility. This was almost identical to Mickey's approach. Goodwin realized that race fans would spend more money in a comfortable environment, such as a sports stadium, with its easy parking and better amenities for the fans. Ultimately, Goodwin was the initiator of the motorcycle racing sport called "Super Motocross." This was a type of indoor motorcycle racing with numerous jumps on a dirt surface, in a large field with riders all starting at the same time. It required the riders to be more technical and rhythmic while gliding around a winding racecourse.

The motorcycle craze grew as new brands came on the market such as Suzuki, Yamaha, Kawasaki, and Honda, which changed young people's thinking about motorcycles. It was no longer a 'hog world' with bulky, hefty Harley Davidsons, which were fixated on comfort and not power and versatility. The new models of Japanese bikes changed motorcycle speed racing and cross-country racing. Now there were thousands of spectators who enjoyed the excitement of motorcycle racing with all the roaring engines, squealing tires, and the stench of exhaust in the air. His Super Motocross events were so popular that they filled the Los Angeles Coliseum with more spectators than football fans attending a UCLA vs. USC game. This was extraordinary for arena events.

Even though both Goodwin and Mickey were in the same business and had some similar traits, there were pronounced differences. Both men's approaches were dissimilar because of their track record in past events. Mickey's past accomplishments from his racing days and his name recognition had become a household name because of all the publicity he received from his auto parts and tire business. Mickey also had been doing stadium racing for much longer and at more sites throughout the country.

When Mickey approached any stadium in the country in regards to scheduling an event, he was welcomed with open arms because he had gained a reputation for being a straight shooter. Besides bringing huge amounts of money to the stadiums, he was also known for keeping his word about cleaning up the stadium after the events. Removing all the dirt without damaging the stadium floor was important to the stadium operators. For Mickey, his word was his bond and stadiums liked working with him to the point that stadium administrators often didn't require him to put down a large security deposit for the use of the stadium. What this meant for his company, MTEG, was that he didn't have to provide $100,000 to be held by various stadiums for security.

Mickey was the envy of all the stadium event promoters. Mickey could afford to spend more on advertising an event, which brought in more paying spectators. On the other hand, Michael Goodwin was one of those jealous promoters who had to continually put up large sums for security deposits, which was costly for any promoter. Goodwin complained to the stadiums that he should be treated the same way Mickey was treated and trusted. The stadiums' operators listened, and their only reply to Goodwin was, "You're not Mickey Thompson." Goodwin resented being treated that way, since he believed that Mickey had taken, or in his mind, stolen some of Goodwin's ideas in the staging of stadium events. Goodwin candidly believed that Mickey owed him, and it hurt to be considered inferior when negotiating with the stadiums.

(This graphic page shows Michael Goodwin & his career.)

MICHAEL GOODWIN

Concert Promoter for the Carpenters

Concert Promoter for Janis Joplin

Promoter of Motocross

Promoter of Super Cross

Arrested for defrauding bank

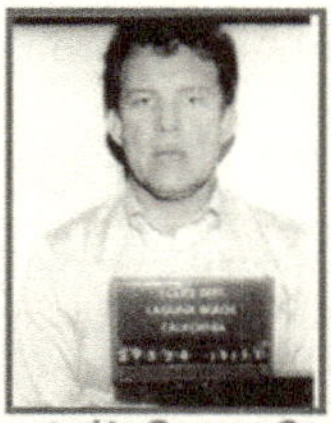

Arrested in Orange County

Goodwin's classic car

Media pool photos of Goodwin during Trial in Pasadena

CHAPTER 15. PARTNERSHIP IS FORMED

It was hard to say whether Goodwin was envious or resentful of the favoritism Mickey received from the stadium operators. Some of the stadiums had proposed the idea that if the promoters combined their resources, they could use the same venue to put on both big truck and motorcycle racing events. The logic was that both types of events required huge amounts of dirt to be brought in and spread all over the floor of a stadium. Inevitably, after the event, all the dirt had to be removed. All this dirt moving was extremely costly. If they could stage their events on consecutive days, such as one on a Saturday and the other on a Sunday, they would have the best of all possible worlds.

It was highly beneficial for both Goodwin and Mickey to combine their resources to use a particular venue for both auto and motorcycle racing. The question was how to structure an agreement that both of them could live with. Because of Trudy's health problems, Mickey didn't want to burden her with the actual daily operation. He wanted Goodwin to take that lead. Mickey's main contribution would be the use of his name to gain recognition for the events and assure the facilities and vendors that all the expenses would be paid.

Combining both of their operations made sense and would save them money; after all, they both appealed to the same types of race fans. It appeared like a good match. By March 30, 1984, both Mickey and Goodwin were able to come up with a partnership agreement that seemed like a perfect arrangement for both of them, one which subsequently would make both of them richer than rich.

The partnership was structured so that 70% of the business belonged to Goodwin and a lesser 30% owned by Mickey. Goodwin would get an annual salary of $300,000, and Mickey would receive a much smaller salary. There was a back out clause for Goodwin after 18 months. This arrangement was fine for Mickey, who didn't want to be as involved in the actual business decisions and was glad to give that responsibility to Goodwin. The other side of the agreement was that Mickey would have to put up only 30% of the expenses for an event and Goodwin would have to put up 70%, which was the bulk of the money. The profits would be divided in the same proportion. Mickey didn't want any misunderstanding about the partnership, so he had his attorney draw up the wording for the agreement. After going through several drafts, Mickey realized he had the most at stake since his name would be used by Goodwin. He was proud of his accomplishments in which his name 'Mickey Thompson Racing Event' could automatically generate thousands of dollars in revenue sales.

Goodwin may have gone into this partnership with another agenda. It wasn't clear what his objective was in agreeing to the partnership. He had looked upon Mickey as his competition and rival, so to him the partnership agreement was a way to eliminate Mickey as a threat or a challenge. Some insight into Goodwin's thinking was supplied by Charles Stewart Letterman (pseudonym) who worked for Goodwin's company "In Sport." He held various positions for Goodwin, and on the date both Goodwin and Mickey were to sign the partnership agreement, Mr. Letterman's job was to drive Goodwin and the president of his company, Jeannie Sweeney (pseudonym), to Mickey's attorney's office in downtown Los Angeles. After the meeting, Mr. Letterman drove them back to their office in Orange County. During the drive back, Goodwin, in a loud resentful voice, ranted and raved how he was going to rip off Mickey. With glee, he related he had Mickey where he wanted him and the signing of the partnership agreement had changed everything. The other person in the car didn't say much but just listened to Goodwin's rambling on how he was going to take advantage of Mickey. Finally, when they reached the office, Goodwin turned to Mr. Letterman, the driver, and said. "Stu, if you say one word about this, I'll kill you."

This insight into Goodwin's mindset indicated the partnership wasn't built on a solid foundation. Mickey and Trudy were unaware of what they had just entered into. Within months, they would be blindsided by the true intentions of Goodwin as a result of this new partnership.

CHAPTER 16. DISSOLVING OF PARTNERSHIP

Just like in marriages, the honeymoon doesn't last forever. In this case, the marriage between Mickey and Goodwin only lasted for several months. Jointly, they put on three events in the Midwest, and they all lost money. It was never clear what caused the unprofitability of these events. Was the low attendance due to bad weather conditions that kept spectators away? Or could it have been due to a lack of promotional advertising? Since Mickey was no longer involved in the daily operations, he wasn't aware that anything had gone wrong. Mickey was contacted by Goodwin to deposit a total of more than $200,000 to cover bills, and Mickey assumed that Goodwin was depositing even more, reflecting his 70% ownership.

Mickey soon discovered that Goodwin wasn't making any deposits and the bills weren't being paid. By then, Goodwin had stopped providing Mickey with the financial reports of the business. The extent of the losses was totally unknown to Mickey. Goodwin's response to all of these losses was that in the partnership agreement; Mickey was to cover all losses related to **car** events.

Immediately, Mickey was contacted by the stadiums and vendors asking to be paid. This was a surprise to Mickey since his events seldom ever lost money. Mickey had never been in a position where the venues came after him, like bill collectors, asking to be paid. This enraged him since his reputation was that he always paid his bills on time.

Mickey contacted Goodwin and asked why these bills hadn't been paid. Goodwin's reply was the events hadn't been successful and no profit had been made at those venues. This shocked Mickey since it didn't matter whether a profit was made or not; you still paid your expenses.

In the end, Mickey paid $515,000 out of his own pocket to pay the bills and then turned to Goodwin for a refund to him. Goodwin refused to pay and said that he would not reimburse Mickey a dime. After that, Mickey was furious, and all he could think about was dissolving the partnership and severing his ties with Goodwin. The partnership lasted a mere four months. Mickey was a man of his word, and he expected Goodwin to keep his word to pay his share of the expenses. Mickey was a man who wasn't used to losing. Goodwin may not have realized who he had just double-crossed. Mickey came from the old school in which he didn't **FORGIVE OR FORGET.**

CHAPTER 17. BITTER LAWSUIT

That was the beginning of one of the most acrimonious feuds in all of sports business history. But neither man wanted to lose, at least in the eyes of the business public. They didn't want to appear weak or be thought of as a failure. It has been said that both men were willing to spend more than a million dollars in attorneys' fees so they could give the appearance of being the winner of this legal battle. Here were two grown men fighting over $514,388. This amount was no more than pocket change to either of them. Mickey brought a lawsuit to force Goodwin to pay the amount owed. Every step of the way Goodwin vigorously fought the lawsuit, claiming it was Mickey who was to pay for the losses from the car racing events. This wasn't ever mentioned in the negotiation of the agreement, and it certainly wasn't spelled out in the partnership contract. As a result, Goodwin continued to lose in court every step of the way up through the Appellate Court system.

Every time Goodwin lost, he would appeal until he went all the way up to the U.S. Supreme Court. This was the end of the line since there was nowhere else to appeal to. Again, Mickey won and Goodwin was liable for the full amount, which now included interest on the judgment and had risen to over $793,069.40. Just when everyone thought the lawsuits were over, it was merely just the beginning of more problems.

As much as Mickey liked to win, Goodwin hated to lose even more. In order to make sure that Mickey never collected a dime on the judgment, Goodwin went to the extreme of declaring **business** bankruptcy. By doing that, Mickey might win the lawsuit, but he would also lose since he would never be able to collect any money from Goodwin. Mickey's attorneys tried to pierce the corporate veil of Goodwin's corporation, in which they were successful and paved the way for Mickey to collect from Goodwin. In order to prevent that, Goodwin immediately declared **personal** bankruptcy, which meant Mickey wouldn't be able to collect anything from him. At that moment, Goodwin believed he was bulletproof and had checkmated Mickey from ever collecting on his judgment against him.

The lawsuit wasn't the only way to snare the other. Mickey went on a campaign to obtain exclusive agreements for racing events at both Anaheim Stadium and the Rose Bowl. These were venues that Goodwin had been able to use for years. But Goodwin losing the use of the Anaheim Stadium for his racing events was catastrophic since it was his biggest money maker. Goodwin was definitely on the losing end. So, to take revenge, Goodwin took out advertisements stating that Mickey's event had been canceled. When the ticket sales for the event evaporated, Mickey's people realized what had happened. Mickey had his attorney immediately go to court to obtain an injunction to prevent Goodwin from running such ads. The two titans kept going after each other.

When it seemed like it was definitely over, attorneys from the other side would think of another avenue of attack. This time Mickey went into the bankruptcy court to have his judgment he had won to be exempt from Goodwin's bankruptcy. The law stated that bankruptcy can't discharge debts involving fraud. Mickey's attorneys were successful in proving the fraud, and now Mickey could collect his money by garnishing or seizing any asset owned by Goodwin.

One might think that this business feud had turned personal. That's not the half of it. In February 1988, it was going to become even more personal. Just as the court ruled in Mickey's favor, Mickey decided it was time to take off the "kid gloves." He wanted to impose some pain on Goodwin for his refusal to cooperate. The one thing that Goodwin cherished most was his classic Mercedes, which he had loaded with exotic extras that he enjoyed driving around town in. This car was Goodwin's pride and joy. So Mickey, through the bankruptcy trustee, had the Marshal's Office go to Goodwin's house and seize his beloved Mercedes. When Deputy Marshal was having the tow truck hook up Goodwin's Mercedes, Goodwin said, "Mickey doesn't know who he's fucking with. He's fucking dead." It took Goodwin several weeks before he got his beloved car back from the Marshal's Office.

This was just a little sample of the animosity between these two very successful businessmen. A week or so later, Goodwin received more bad news when his counter lawsuit against Mickey was thrown out of court. By this time, Goodwin had exhausted all of his legal options. How was he going to prevent Mickey from winning? He could try one last time to negotiate a settlement, and if that didn't work out, he could fraudulently obtain as much money as possible and then make an exodus from the country.

This plan to abscond from the country with his assets would allow him to live well somewhere else, as well as prevent Mickey from collecting on the judgment. Even though Goodwin believed this would make him the ultimate winner, it seemed like a hollow victory, since he would have to live undercover and wouldn't be able to continue his business. Goodwin thought he could only be declared the winner if he could force Mickey to suffer more pain than he was suffering. What could he do to inflict the most agonizing pain on Mickey?

(The following graphic page shows the Partnership Agreement that was dissolved and that led to endless lawsuits.)

Graphic 13

LAWSUITS BETWEEN MICKEY & GOODWIN

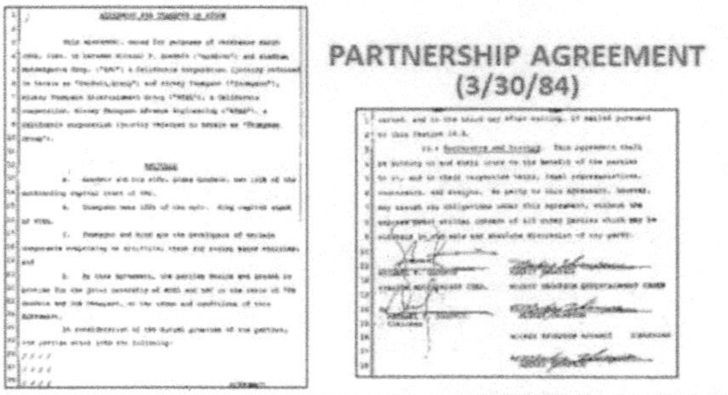

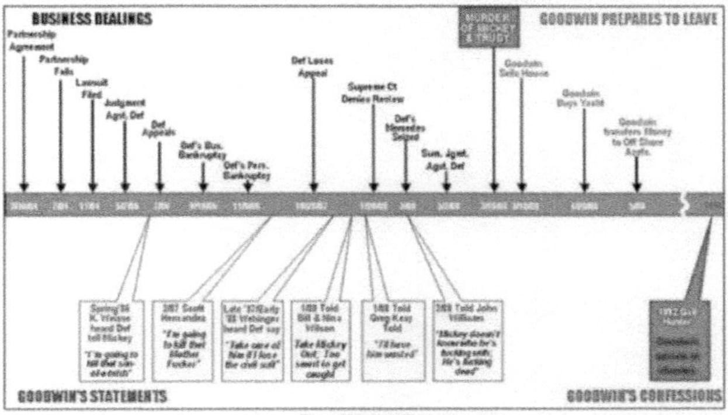

Timeline of Events

Civil Lawsuits between Thompson & Goodwin

CHAPTER 18. Goodwin's Diabolical Plan

March of 1988 was a pivotal point in the Thompson-Goodwin grudge match. Mickey had won all the lawsuits, and with the legal judgment he was actively seizing anything that had Goodwin's name on it. Goodwin didn't like playing the role of the beaten warrior. What could Goodwin do to Mickey in retaliation for all suffering that Mickey had put him through? Mickey's seizing of Goodwin's pride-and joy-Mercedes had been so humiliating. Goodwin tried to think of what Mickey held dearly. Mickey possessed so many cars that losing a car wouldn't cause him any real discomfort.

There weren't any physical possessions Mickey had that couldn't be replaced. Mickey cherished his reputation, and there wasn't anything Goodwin could do to tarnish it. However, everyone knew that Mickey's greatest love was his wife, Trudy. She meant everything to him. Mickey knew that without her steady influence and pleasing personality he would never have attained the degree of success he had experienced. He was so indebted to Trudy for helping him bounce back from the boating accident that had temporarily left him paralyzed.

After much reflection, Michael Goodwin conceived the most sinister scheme that would impose the most severe pain on Mickey. Goodwin's plan was to force Mickey to watch his wife plead for her life and then kill her before Mickey's eyes. This would cause Mickey to feel so helpless, seeing his wife suffer death in front of him. Following her murder, Mickey would be likewise executed.

Goodwin prided himself on being an incredibly shrewd and clever individual. He knew the only way he would be considered the winner of the Thompson-Goodwin feud was if he were able to get away with these murders. So he developed a diabolical scheme in which Mickey and Trudy would be killed at their home when they were leaving for work. However, to make sure that he wouldn't be suspected, he hired two black men who would actually do the murders and escape on bicycles. If they were spotted riding away, the eyewitnesses would report that the suspects appeared to be black and in no way resembled Goodwin's description.

The actual murder plan required considerable preparation and a high degree of sophistication. Mickey's house was easily accessible to the public since the driveway was not within the gated walls of the City of Bradbury. Goodwin knew where Mickey lived, but he was not familiar with the streets surrounding the area. Mickey was one of the most predictable persons since he was an early riser and went to the office at the exact same time every day. Goodwin knew precisely where Mickey and Trudy would be at 6:00 a.m. every workday. They would be leaving for work as they always did.

It was easy for Goodwin to figure out where Mickey and Trudy would be at that precise time in the morning. Later in the day, their schedule might vary depending on meetings and traffic congestion on the 57 Freeway coming out of Anaheim Stadium. Also, doing the shooting early in the morning would keep the number of possible eyewitnesses to a minimum. But the real challenge was to find a way for the gunmen to escape. Anyone who looks at Mt. Olive Drive, which runs next to the

Thompson house, would quickly realize that it was the only route of escape from the house. This posed a problem for the shooters in that the Sheriff's Department could block that road off at the bottom of the hill, preventing any escape by the shooters.

That was assuming that the shooters were driving a motor vehicle. If the shooters were to use bicycles, they could ride through the City of Bradbury and exit by the south gate. This was a brilliant plan since the responding deputies would be assuming a motor vehicle was involved. The other benefit was that when the shooters left by the south gate, they could exit through a small hole in the fence that led to the regional bicycle path that went for miles in either direction. Within minutes, they could meet up with their getaway vehicle, throw their bikes in the back, and drive off on the 210 Freeway, where they would blend in with the thousands of commuters on their way to work.

The shooting and the escape were well thought out; all that was left was how to provide a rock-solid alibi for Goodwin. Since he was a member of the Irvine sports gym, he could visit the gym around 5:30 a.m. and talk to numerous people as he pretended to be working out. This would provide him with reliable alibi witnesses who could recall talking to Michael Goodwin at the gym. Goodwin knew as soon as Mickey's death was ascertained by the Sheriff's Department and news media, they would be trying to track him down for a statement.

The best way to handle law enforcement and the media was to surround himself with his attorney, who would be the spokesperson for him. Once the homicide detectives were told he had an attorney who was handling the matter, they would have to back off from trying to get him to talk. But his attorney would have to provide a reason why he didn't want to talk. The perfect excuse was that he was in fear for his life from the same people who had killed Mickey and his wife. This reasoning didn't seem to be based on logic or common sense. The public, who didn't know about the bitter lawsuits, might buy into this explanation as to why Goodwin wanted to stay undercover and not accessible.

All the while, his attorney would express how much Goodwin wanted to cooperate but was doing this to protect himself and his wife, Diane. He was so afraid of the killers that he was going to leave the Southern California area. In fact, on the night of the shooting, he traveled to the Las Vegas area to stay with friends, claiming that he was trying to make it hard for Mickey's killers to track him down.

CHAPTER 19. LEAVING THE COUNTRY

From the time just before the killings to six weeks after, Goodwin and his wife were involved in deceitful activity as they moved their assets to offshore banks while purchasing a new yacht. Since Goodwin had filed for bankruptcy, his assets were supposedly tied up in the bankruptcy court. However, within days of the murders, Goodwin and Diane sold their Laguna Beach house that they had been living in. Documents indicated that the sale occurred two days before the murders, although the escrow papers were signed two days after the murders. It wasn't clear whether the sale price had been substantially reduced to expedite the sale. Their house had been on the market for months without any serious buyers. Ironically, around the time of the murders the house quickly sold, suggesting that Goodwin might have been motivated to sell since he wanted to leave the area.

Several suspicious business transactions also occurred when Goodwin immediately sold two separate investment properties. Any proceeds from the sale of those investments were to be given to the bankruptcy receiver. However, Goodwin and his wife Diane were able to sell off the investments and have the money deposited in Diane's personal bank accounts. From there she and Goodwin went to a local coin store, where they purchased a large quantity of Krugerrands.

These gold coins were originally issued by the South African government starting in 1967 and were very popular in the 1980s. People who were concerned about a country's currency could put their money into Krugerrands, which was like possessing pure gold. Although the actual bullion coins aren't made up of pure gold, they do contain 91.67 % pure gold, and 8.33% is made up of copper. The reason for the addition of the copper was to make the coin more durable and resistant to scratching. However, each coin still contained one troy ounce of pure gold. Later it was minted privately and looked the same except for a country's name was absent.

The Goodwins purchased the Krugerrand gold coins partly with the funds they had obtained from the sale of their investments. The advantage of the Krugerrands was they could easily be converted into currency in any country. Diane made two purchases of these Krugerrands on different dates and paid for them from her personal bank account. The Goodwins also transferred some of their remaining funds into bank accounts in the Turks, Caicos, and Grand Cayman Islands.

At this point, Goodwin and his wife had sold their house, established an offshore bank account to live off, and possessed a large quantity of Krugerrands they could use to sustain their travels and support their lifestyle. At the same time, they had to find a new place to live. Shortly before the murders, Goodwin and his wife had gone on trips to the east coast to look for a large sailboat yacht they could purchase. Because of the bankruptcy, Goodwin wouldn't have been able to purchase an expensive yacht in his name. So, Goodwin had the yacht purchased in Diane's name by financing it through a Maryland bank. They both fraudulently misrepresented their financial situation. Without the Maryland bank knowing the true nature of their financial condition, the bank approved the loan for the purchase the yacht. Goodwin spent additional money fitting the boat with certain custom features that would permit them to live on it comfortably.

Although Goodwin and his wife had looked for a boat before the murders, it wasn't until after the murders that they were able to secure the purchase of a 57-foot Wellington Motor Sailor yacht named 'Rebel Venture III' for $400,000. The yacht was the perfect place to live. They had no address and no ties to the United States. They were free to live anywhere they could navigate their boat. They could sail all over the Caribbean without worrying about being tracked down by law enforcement. They could move from port to port. When they needed money, they could go to any bank and convert some of their Krugerrands into the local currency or have funds wired to them from their bank accounts in the Cayman Islands.

By May of 1988, Michael and Diane Goodwin had permanently moved onto their yacht and had sailed off into the sunset. Should the fact that Goodwin and his wife left town be considered an act of 'Consciousness of Guilt' on their part? Or was this an act of a man who was in fear for his life trying to hide from whoever was out to harm him and his wife? Since they didn't actually leave town for six weeks, would that still be considered 'flight after a crime'?

Goodwin having left for the Caribbean made it more difficult for the detectives to investigate whether or not he had been involved in the killings. It also made it more problematic for anyone to find him if they were out to harm him. It was challenging to trace Goodwin's movements since he was careful not to leave a trail. The two of them continued to enjoy the good life as fugitives on the run for nearly two years. They sailed in and out of the Caribbean Islands without creating any attention to their boat. For boat people, they had a perfect life, and there was plenty of money to handle their limited overhead. They could move from one gorgeous island to another and tie up each evening at any inviting inlet. They could visit any yacht club and socialize with other seafarers, like themselves, while enjoying a refreshing drink or two. Mornings were pleasant with no early rising to get to work on time or a hectic commute to an office. They could eat at any time they wanted and had the option of fresh fish by merely throwing a fishing line into the crystal-clear water, or they could buy something from the local markets. This was the life that many dream of and *believe* they will have for their retirement, and maybe that was why they changed the name of their boat to 'BELIEVE.'

As idyllic as life seemed for Goodwin and his wife, there may have been some friction that developed between the two of them. It was not known what triggered it, but Michael Goodwin sailed into a harbor of a small Caribbean island. His wife, Diane, jumped off the boat onto the dock in order to tie up the boat. Goodwin then thrust the engine into reverse and backed the boat out to sea, leaving his wife stranded with nothing but the bikini she was wearing. She was left to fend for herself without a passport or money.

Most people would find this to be the most loathsome act imaginable. This story is hard to verify since Diane and Goodwin never wanted to talk about it. What is known as a fact is that they parted company on one of the Caribbean Islands, which marked the end of their serene and, as some would say, blissful life together cruising the isles of paradise.

Goodwin, without Diane, continued to sail down to Central America. For whatever reason, Goodwin changed the name of the boat this time to 'SCALAWAG.' In the meantime, the Maryland Bank was earnestly trying to track him down since they hadn't received any payments on the loan they had made to Diane Goodwin. When they checked out the paperwork the Goodwins had signed, the bankers realized they had been defrauded, in that the Goodwins didn't have any assets left in the USA. Sometime in 1990, the Maryland Bank had assigned private investigators to locate the boat and the Goodwins. They were able to trace the 'Scalawag' down to ports near Guatemala. The private investigators met up with Goodwin in a bar and explained they were there to get the boat. Goodwin stated, in no uncertain terms, "Don't touch my boat." Soon thereafter, Goodwin sailed away on the boat.

A short time later, repossessors spotted the boat and waited for Goodwin to go ashore. When Goodwin was away, the repossessors did what they are good at doing and seized the boat. When Goodwin returned, he was surprised to find that his beloved 'Scalawag' yacht had mysteriously disappeared. After the bank finally acquired the boat back, it was practically destroyed, since little maintenance had been done while Goodwin was sailing the seas. Without a sailboat and without Diane supplying money, Goodwin was forced to return to the United States.

(The following graphic page shows documents of the yacht purchase and how the Goodwins were able to move assets out of the country while in bankruptcy.)

Graphic 14

GOODWIN LEAVING COUNTRY

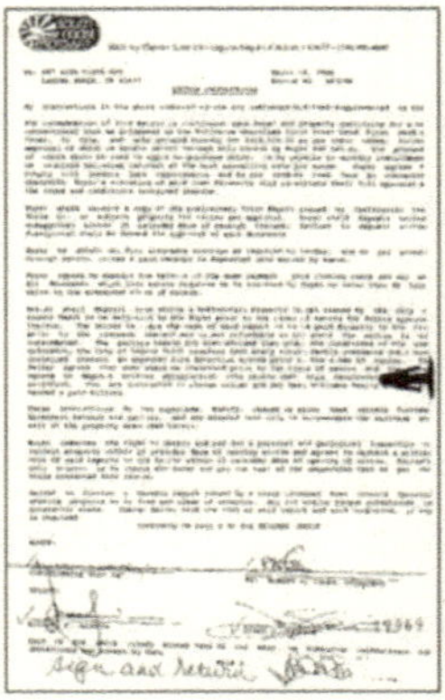

Escrow Instructions for selling house 3/18/88

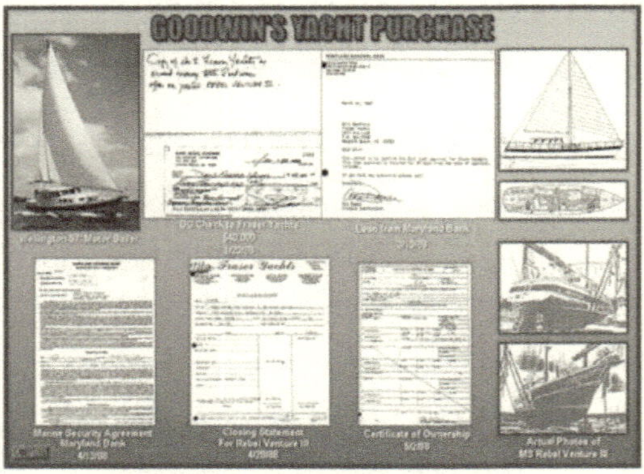

Documents showing the purchase of Wellington 57' Motorsailer

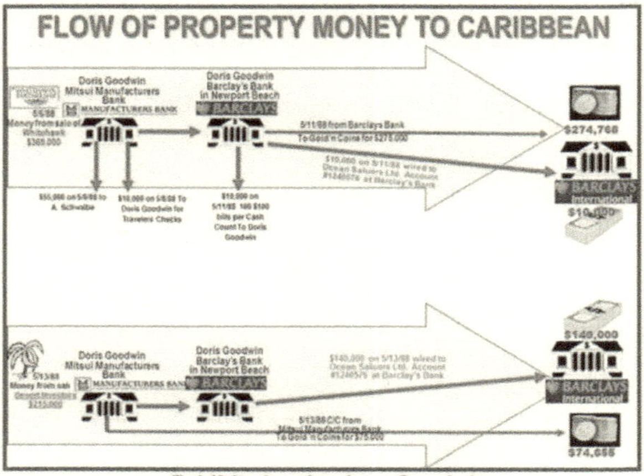

Exhibit showing how Goodwin transferred finds while in Bankruptcy

CHAPTER 20. GOODWIN RETURNS TO USA

The money was drying up for Goodwin, and his financial problems were mounting. His arrival in the USA didn't attract any attention from authorities. He needed to maintain a low profile, especially from the Maryland Bank, the Federal Bankruptcy Court, and the Los Angeles Sheriff's Department. Upon his return, he headed for Aspen, Colorado, to mix with the rich and famous. The early 1990s saw a recession set in to slow the economy, making jobs scarce to come by. Goodwin needed to find some way or someone who would be willing to support him. In Aspen, he frequented the trendy bars. There he met Gail Monahan (pseudonym) at a ski cocktail lounge. She was the owner of an art gallery in town and certainly would be ranked in the upper crust of Aspen. Goodwin ingratiated himself to Gail, who was having some problems of her own. Within a short time, the two were living together at Gail's place, which was a cozy mountain retreat. They seemed to hit it off well for several years starting in 1990.

After they had been living together for some time, one night Goodwin told Gail to watch a videotape he had copied titled, "Unsolved Mysteries." The program was about the murders of Mickey and Trudy Thompson and how the killers had never been caught. Goodwin kept telling Gail, "Look what I've done, and I got away with it." He just couldn't stop talking about the program and how smart he was. He bragged about the fact that he had hired two black teenagers to carry out the assassination. Goodwin seemed to be obsessed with looking at this video incessantly.

Listening to Goodwin talk about the tape and his constant viewing of it made her think that he was definitely involved in the Thompsons' murders. She didn't reveal any of this to anyone because she was in deadly fear of Goodwin. He always had a gun next to the bed and told her if she told anyone that she wouldn't survive. As time went by, the couple's relationship deteriorated. By the end of 1992, Gail was hospitalized with serious injuries inflicted by Goodwin. The police investigated a possible domestic violence, and as a result, Goodwin's whereabouts became known to the authorities. Since Gail didn't want to bring charges against Goodwin, they split and went their separate ways.

By 1993, Goodwin reappeared in the U.S. District Court in Santa Ana for a hearing on a dispute related to his bankruptcy. Then the FBI had him arrested for federal bankruptcy fraud. Shortly afterward, the federal prosecutors dropped the charges and he was a free man. He had to feel quite comfortable that he wasn't charged with any bankruptcy violations and especially no charges of homicide. For the next two years, he appeared invincible from the grasp of authorities.

However, the Maryland Bank didn't like being defrauded, and they wouldn't give up. They wanted Goodwin and his wife prosecuted for lying about their assets when they applied for the loan to purchase the sailboat. By the fall of 1995, a federal grand jury was investigating allegations that Goodwin had lied about his financial situation. The irony was at that exact time there was a federal government shutdown in which an intern by the name of Monica Lewinsky, who was helping then-President Bill Clinton run the government from the oval office. Later the president would be caught up in a comparable lie during an impeachment proceeding.

Nonetheless, Goodwin's lie apparently was more serious since it pertained to a financial matter, and the Grand Jury indicted him and his former wife, Diane, with 13 counts of making false statements on a bank application to finance their business and buy a yacht. When the Goodwins applied for the $400,000 loan, they failed to disclose that they hadn't repaid a prior loan. Also, they didn't reveal that they had sold their assets amounting to about $500,000, which they then used to purchase 700 Krugerrand gold coins. They were both tried before a federal jury, and were convicted of defrauding two separate financial institutions. Both Goodwin and Diane were sentenced to 30 months in federal prison. It seemed strange that Goodwin wasn't smart enough to get away with making fraudulent statements on a credit application, but, at the same time, he appeared to be smart enough to get away with a double homicide.

CHAPTER 21. Viewing the Case with Fresh Eyes

In 1989, the Mickey and Trudy Thompson murders were featured on the program "Unsolved Mysteries." The Sheriff's Department worked with the TV program with the hope that more publicity would generate new witnesses that could be used to help solve this double homicide. Later in the year, the Thompson murders were featured again on TV. Both times nothing new was uncovered. The case continued to grow older, and the public started to lose interest in the case that defied closure. Mickey's sister, Colleen Campbell, wouldn't admit defeat. Her background was in local politics serving at various times on the city council and being the mayor of the City of San Juan Capistrano in Orange County, California. She was well known in her community. Being in politics, she was a pragmatist and understood that you don't win every battle, but you never give up the fight, no matter how impossible it might seem.

Colleen's son was unfortunately killed in a drug deal that went terribly wrong. As a result, she became involved with victims' rights groups. This gave her a platform to encourage law enforcement to keep trying to solve murder cases to bring some sort of closure for the victim's families. Whenever she had the opportunity, she would confront law enforcement and prosecutors to encourage them to work on her brother's murder case. As the years went by, she unrelentingly made pleas for continual investigation. Colleen, at her own expense, hired private investigators to follow up on clues and would turn over any information she discovered to authorities. She was convinced that Michael Goodwin was behind the murders and wanted him thoroughly investigated.

She had received from so many people information that Goodwin had a strong motive to kill Mickey and Trudy. Colleen also understood that money can make people talk. So out of her own pocket she set up a reward of $1,000,000 for any information leading to an arrest and conviction of the parties involved. Even with the reward money, there wasn't anything useful generated except for some rumors and hearsay, which couldn't be used in court. Seasons came and went away while the years blurred together without any arrest for the planning and shooting of the Thompsons.

The original detectives retired and had hung up their gun belts. The Sheriff's Department transferred the old Thompson files over to the Cold Case unit. There, a young hot dog homicide detective by the name of Det. Mark Lillienfeld was given the assignment of looking into the unsolved Thompson case. His reputation included being super tenacious. Cocky and sure of his instincts were words people used to describe him. He could assimilate a huge amount of facts, mentally analyze them, and cull out the workable leads. Bureaucratic red tape never seemed to get in his way. He combined his persistence with basic common sense. No one ever accused him of being shy or unable to express his opinions. He conversed in a dialect of folksy talk, occasionally sprinkling in salty language to make his point.

Throughout the 1990s there was renewed interest in “Cold Cases” because of the increased success of using DNA to identify individuals. There were a number of old cases that were being solved by retesting the aging evidence and adding more people into the DNA databases. This hope re-energized the Thompson case, which was one of the most famous unsolved cases in the ‘Cold Case’ file cabinet. Det. Lillienfeld and his fellow detectives looked at all the evidence to see if there was anything that could be re-examined or reanalyzed by the crime lab for possible DNA. Unfortunately, in the Thompson case, there was little in the way of physical evidence found at the crime scene that could be tested for DNA.

All the blood at the crime scene was either from Mickey or Trudy. It appeared unlikely that either one of the shooters had been injured, thus eliminating the possibility of any DNA being left at the crime scene either from suspects’ blood or bodily fluids. The only two items that might have some DNA on them were the stun gun and the orange peels. The stun gun had been carefully examined earlier for fingerprints. Its handle had been wrapped with some type of adhesive tape. Dusting it for prints had been done numerous times. After more than a decade, the stun gun was in no condition to reveal any DNA from anyone who might have used it.

The only remaining hope was the orange peels that had been seen a short distance from Mickey’s body. Elizabeth Divine was the CSI member who was assigned to the case and had arrived at the crime scene between 9:00 a.m. and 9:30 a.m. in the morning. The main focus of her investigation was the blood pool and blood spatter. However, she did notice the orange peels looked fresh since they hadn’t shriveled up or dried around the edges. What was interesting to her was the fact the peelings appeared to have been cut, not torn open by anyone’s fingers. There was the possibility that one of the shooters had peeled the orange while lying in wait to attack Mickey and his wife. There was a possibility that the suspect's saliva could have been transferred onto the orange peels. If that had happened, it could reveal the DNA of that suspect, even if it had been more than a decade since the murders. The investigators looked everywhere, but no one could find the orange peels. The criminalist who had been at the crime scene remembered seeing and examining the peels. It appeared that the orange peels had not been booked into evidence. Even though the criminalist thought it might be of some significance, the detectives at the scene might not have deemed it worthy enough to preserve.

No one knew what happened to the lost orange peels. Back in 1988, the orange peels wouldn't have been thought to contain much in the way of any evidentiary value. DNA testing was a mere pie in the sky at the time. One can only speculate what those orange peels might have revealed. They may have contained one of the suspect's DNA. However, that would be useless evidence unless one knew whose DNA to compare it to. Not until a suspect's DNA is entered into a database can there ever be a match. But for the sake of argument let's presume the orange peels had the saliva from one of the suspects and assume his DNA had been entered into the DNA database. As a result, if someone examined both and ran a test of the DNA against the DNA database and found there to be a match, at least the detectives would know the name of one of the shooters. Even if all that were found to be true, the next big step would be whether that person would still be alive or whether he could be tracked down. If he could be, would he be willing to reveal who hired him to kill Mickey Thompson and his wife?

The detectives wanted to review all the evidence and see if there may have been some other reason for the murders. They checked out the possibility of a romantic triangle by talking to the friends and family of both Mickey and Trudy. There wasn't the slightest bit of evidence to suggest anything unsavory had been going on. Next, they checked out the possibility of drug activity, but several people came forth to explain how much Mickey objected to drug usage. At one event, Mickey grabbed two druggies and picked them up by their collars and told them to get out of the racing area. Mickey didn't have any desire to be involved with the drug scene, nor did he have any sympathy for those who were.

Some rumors surfaced that indicated Mickey was in need of money. The detectives tried to find any evidence that the killing might be the result of loan sharking. His attorneys did say that Mickey was cash poor, but he could obtain funds from any commercial bank if he needed money. Lastly, there was the possibility of being a victim of a robbery. There had been reports that Mickey had come into possession of over $200,000, either in cash or gold. It was alleged that one of Mickey's employees had stated to someone that Mickey had just received a large amount of cash that he may have placed in one of his home safes. When the employee was asked about the money matter, he denied ever knowing anything about it. Mickey's safes were opened and found to contain no cash or gold. Lastly, when the issue of robbery was analyzed, it didn't add up since they both had over $4,000 in cash between them. Also, Trudy was wearing and had very expensive jewelry in the van worth more than $ 20,000.

CHAPTER 22. NEW WITNESSES SURFACE

The new detectives had to rely on the public coming forth with new names of witnesses who could shed fresh light on this unsolved case. Then in 1997, the detectives were able to have the TV series *America's Most Wanted* feature the facts of the case on one of their episodes. This series had a large following and had been instrumental in solving many old cases. Generally, the program concentrated on locating a known suspect who was on the run. Later in 2001, *America's Most Wanted* was willing to rebroadcast the program about the Thompson murders in the hope that something new might be uncovered.

The rebroadcasting of the program was a major break, in a very convoluted way. After one of the TV shows, Det. Lillienfeld heard from a person in Colorado who claimed he had a friend who indicated that he had seen something suspicious several days before the Thompson murders. This seemed so farfetched that it certainly didn't merit wasting investigative time on it. Nevertheless, the detectives were more than eager for any new leads, so they went to all the trouble of trying to track down the one person who might have seen something. Det. Lillienfeld used his stellar investigative skills to hunt down that person, who turned out to be Ronald Johns (pseudonym).

The detective asked him what he knew about the Thompson murders. Mr. Johns said that he didn't see anything in regards to the actual day of the murders. Nevertheless, he did relate that he and his wife had seen something unusual several days before the murders. He didn't know for certain if it had anything to do with the murders, but he had always wanted to talk to someone from the Sheriff's Department to see if there was any connection.

Det. Lillienfeld asked him to explain what he had seen. Mr. Johns related that several days before the murders, around 11:00 a.m., he was returning to his house on Mt. Olive Drive above Gardi Street. His house is located about a quarter mile below the Thompsons' house. As he was approaching his house, he noticed an old station wagon parked on the wrong side of Gardi Street. The car was facing towards him but was against the north curb. This was just south of his horse corral. The driver seemed to be using binoculars to look straight forward in the direction of the school, about a block away. As Mr. Johns pulled into his driveway, he could see his wife and daughter had pulled in just before him. He asked his wife how long those people had been parked in that position. His wife indicated she didn't know since she had just arrived. He told her to call the Sheriff's Department to check it out. In the meantime, he kept looking at the people in the car. From where he was standing, he could see that the driver was a white male with reddish blond hair. He could see that there appeared to be another person on the passenger side of the station wagon, who appeared to be a black male.

Mr. Johns continued to watch for several minutes. Then he decided to approach the car and to better determine what these people were doing in the neighborhood parked on the wrong side of the street. His wife followed behind him to also get a better look at who it might be. He walked up to his corral fence and at that point was about eight feet away, where he could clearly see the man in the driver's seat. The driver turned his head to glance at him and appeared startled. Immediately, he put down the binoculars and started the engine of the old station wagon and quickly drove away. As the car was pulling away, Mrs. Johns could see the license plates and noticed that it appeared to be an Arizona plate.

After the car left, he and his wife tried to figure out what the people might have been doing there. They could have been burglars or 'peeping toms,' trying to case the area. Or, there could have been some innocent reason why they were there. The Johnses soon dismissed the whole affair. Several days later, the Johnses heard about the Thompsons' murders. At that point, they wondered if there was any connection between what they had seen and the murders. Shortly after the homicides, they saw some Sheriff's Deputies in the area. Mr. Johns approached the deputies and told them what he and his wife had seen several days before the killings. Mr. Johns explained that he and his wife had seen a white male and a black male in an old station wagon appearing to be scoping out the area. The deputies said the Sheriff's Department was looking for two black males who had been on bicycles. The deputies didn't seem interested in the information, and the Johnses felt that maybe there wasn't any connection between what happened several days before and the the shootings.

Over the next decade, the Johnses would mention this in casual conversations with friends about their curiosity as to whether the two events were connected. The Johnses' house was at an ideal location to view the comings and goings of anyone at the Thompsons' house. Mickey and Trudy had to travel past the Johnses' place every time they went anywhere from their house. From the Johnses' property, Mt. Olive Drive climbed up a steep incline and curved by the Thompsons' house. Anybody watching from that location could determine when Mickey and Trudy left and came home from work. Mickey's morning schedule was highly predictable, but his nightly routine could vary, depending on social occasions he might have to attend.

CHAPTER 23. LINEUP OF GOODWIN

When Det. Lillienfeld was talking to Ronald Johns, he asked him if he thought he could identify the driver. Mr. Johns said that he might be able to. Det. Lillienfeld had six large posters of similar males, one of which included Michael Goodwin. Mr. Johns slowly looked over all the photos and then picked out the photo of Michael Goodwin. He indicated the photo was the one that looked most like the driver of the station wagon.

In order to determine if Mr. Johns could positively identify Goodwin, the detectives needed to conduct a live lineup. The Sheriff's detectives contacted Goodwin through his attorney and asked him to submit to a lineup. Goodwin's attorney refused to allow Goodwin to participate. The Sheriff's Department ordered him to appear for a lineup on a certain date. Goodwin's attorney went into court to block such an attempt. This matter went all the way up to the Appellate Court. That court agreed with Goodwin that he couldn't be forced to stand in a lineup since he wasn't in custody.

It looked like the courts had blocked any way of having a lineup to determine if the witnesses could identify Goodwin as the person they had seen in the area several days before the murders. Without a lineup, there couldn't be any positive identification; therefore, there couldn't be an arrest of Goodwin. Without an arrest, there wasn't any way the detectives could force Goodwin to stand in a lineup. This was a definite "Catch 22." After a thorough reading of the Appellate Court decision, there appeared to be some weasel language in the Appellate Court opinion in which a person could be required to participate in a lineup.

The court opinion said that if a person was arrested on a "Ramey Warrant," then the person detained could be required to appear in a lineup. The so-called "Ramey Warrant" came about 30 years earlier in the case of People v. Ramey. In that case, the California Supreme Court said that a person couldn't be arrested in his home unless a magistrate had determined there was sufficient probable cause. Up to this point, the district attorney's office had indicated that there wasn't sufficient evidence for a filing of a criminal complaint against Goodwin. The legal standard for filing criminal charges by the prosecutor is much higher than the standard for a mere probable cause arrest done by law enforcement.

Det. Lillienfeld wasn't the type of person who looked for all the reasons why something couldn't be done. He's the sort who would find every obstacle a challenge and not an impediment. He saw that the Appellate Court mentioned the use of a "Ramey Warrant." So in his usual persona, he went to the district attorney's office and asked for a "Ramey Warrant." No one had ever thought of using a "Ramey Warrant" to force a person who was not in custody to stand in a lineup. There was a Deputy District Attorney, Scott Carbaugh, who was familiar with the Mickey

Thompson murder case and had no problem preparing a "Ramey Warrant" for a judge to sign. In short order, the "Ramey Warrant" was signed by Judge John Torribio, and Det. Lillienfeld had what he needed to proceed with the next step of the case.

On Sunday, August 3, 2001, over 13 years after the murders, Michael Goodwin was arrested on a "Ramey Warrant." The Sheriff's Department arranged a lineup at the Los Angeles County Jail for the next day. Det. Lillienfeld arranged for Ron Johns to attend. Since his wife had also seen the stranger, she was invited to come along to see if she could make an identification. Up to this point, only Ron Johns had been shown a group of photos of individuals that included Goodwin. His wife hadn't seen any previous photos of Goodwin, or anyone else. At the lineup, Mr. and Mrs. Johns were seated apart from each other in the audience. They were separated from the stage by a large pane of glass. This prevents those in the lineup from seeing who is in the audience. The investigator in charge of the lineup instructed them as to what they were about to see. They were given a separate sheet of paper to fill out at the end of the lineup. Six individuals were brought out onto the stage and asked to stand in a line. Then each one was asked to turn sideways so their profile could be seen. Then everyone was asked individually to step forward.

Then all the parties in the lineup were given a watch cap (beanie) to wear. They again were asked to step forward and turn sideways. That concluded the live lineup. Afterward, Mr. and Mrs. Johns were asked to fill out the sheet of paper indicating whether they were able to identify anyone in the lineup. Both Mr. and Mrs. Johns separately filled out the sheets stating the person that they had seen scoping out the neighborhood was number 5. That was the number Michael Goodwin was wearing during the lineup. From that point on, the Sheriff's detectives had a positive identification. Then the next question was, what were they going to do with it?

Since the case needed to be updated before it could be presented to the DA's Office, Goodwin was released on the "Ramey Warrant." As he walked out of the County Jail, he clutched a Bible in his hand, as though it had brought him good luck since no charges were being filed against him.

(The following graphic page shows where the Johnses claimed to have seen Goodwin two days before the shooting. Also is shown the lineup in which they identified Goodwin.)

Graphic 15

WITNESS IDENTIFICATION

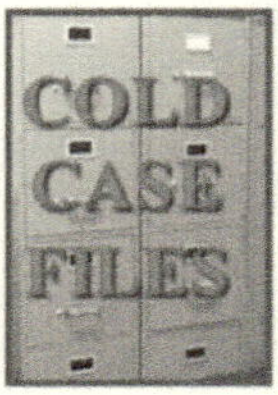

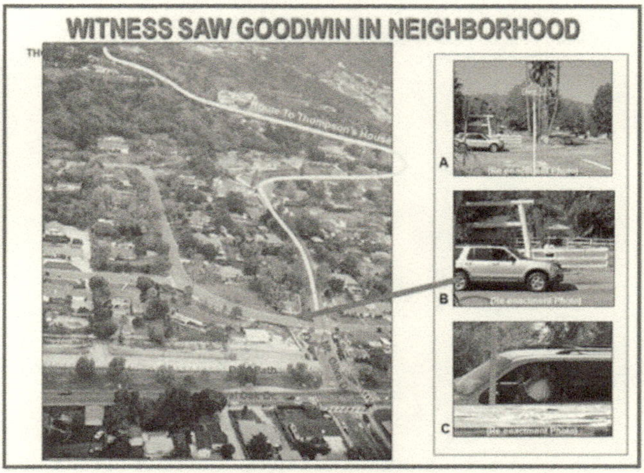

Location where Goodwin was seen two days before shooting

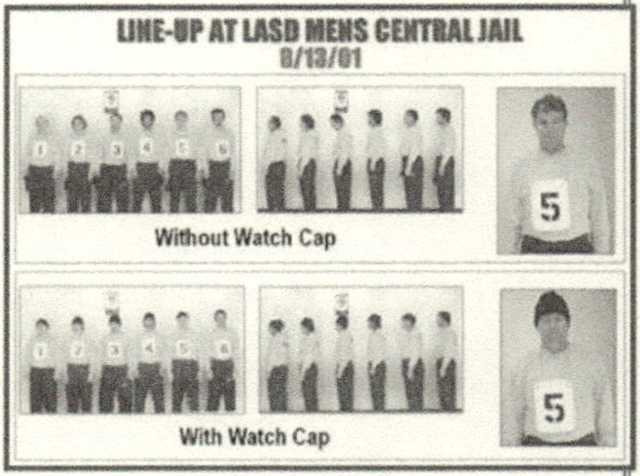

Line-up in Los Angeles where witnesses identified Goodwin

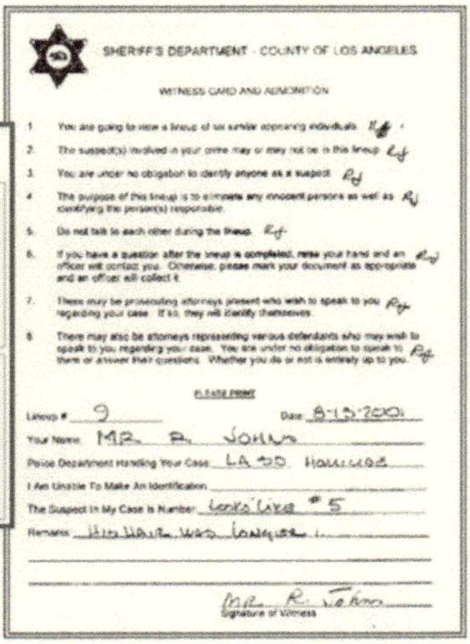

SHERIFF'S DEPARTMENT - COUNTY OF LOS ANGELES

WITNESS CARD AND ADMONITION

1. You are going to view a lineup of six similar appearing individuals. RJ
2. The suspect(s) involved in your crime may or may not be in this lineup. RJ
3. You are under no obligation to identify anyone as a suspect. RJ
4. The purpose of this lineup is to eliminate any innocent persons as well as identifying the person(s) responsible. RJ
5. Do not talk to each other during the lineup. RJ
6. If you have a question after the lineup is completed, raise your hand and an officer will contact you. Otherwise, please mark your document as appropriate and an officer will collect it. RJ
7. There may be prosecuting attorneys present who wish to speak to you regarding your case. If so, they will identify themselves. RJ
8. There may also be attorneys representing various defendants who may wish to speak to you regarding your case. You are under no obligation to speak to them or answer their questions. Whether you do or not is entirely up to you. RJ

PLEASE PRINT

Lineup # 9 Date 8-13-2001

Your Name MR. R. JOHN

Police Department Handling Your Case LASD Homicide

I Am Unable To Make An Identification ____

The Suspect In My Case Is Number Looks Like #5

Remarks His hair was longer.

MR. R. John
Signature of Witness

CHAPTER 24. GOODWIN THREATS

With the identification of Goodwin in the area several days before the shooting, new life was injected into the Thompson case. The detectives knew that by itself, the Johnses' identification wouldn't result in a filing of the case. What was needed was a review of what evidence that still existed and what witnesses could be located. During the investigation, the detectives found many people who indicated they had heard Michael Goodwin make threats to kill Mickey Thompson. The detectives needed to find who those people were and whether they had actually heard Goodwin personally make a threat.

There were plenty of witnesses who could testify in court that Mickey had told them that he was in fear of Goodwin. In the eyes of the law, that is hearsay, in which the declarant (meaning Mickey) was no longer available to be cross-examined by the defendant. This was a strange legal fiction since the declarant, Mickey, was unavailable because of the action of the defendant, Goodwin, who was accused of killing him. In other words, the court won't allow the use, in court, of the words "He threatened to kill me." However, the court would allow the words "I'm going to kill you," if the witnesses came to court and testified the declarant was the defendant who said those words. Even though those words are hearsay, the court allows it because the defendant can cross-examine the witness as to what he heard. Also, such words may qualify as an exception to the hearsay rule if they are found to be admissions or declarations against penal interest.

The detectives realized that they needed to concentrate on locating witnesses who heard Goodwin make the threats against Mickey and not waste their time tracking down witnesses who heard Mickey relating such threats against him, by Goodwin. Originally, the detectives were locating people who had heard rumors that Goodwin hated Mickey. It was hard to pin down someone who had actually heard Goodwin make a threat against Mickey. The detectives knew how important the statements were, so they pursued every lead. They started narrowing down the alleged statements and found there were at least a dozen people who had heard such threats firsthand from Goodwin.

Chronologically, the first such threat was overheard by Kathy Wilton (pseudonym), who had worked for Goodwin. During the spring of 1986, Mickey had obtained a court judgment against Goodwin. She was working as Goodwin's receptionist when one day she received a phone call from Mickey Thompson, who asked to speak to Goodwin. She had told Goodwin that Mickey was on the line. She could hear the two of them conversing, and since Goodwin was using a speakerphone, Kathy Wilton could hear what they were both saying. She could hear Goodwin speaking loudly and being argumentative with Mickey. At one point, she heard Goodwin say to Mickey, "You know I can have you taken out. And I will have you taken out." After the phone call was over, she heard Goodwin say, "It will cost me $500 and a motorcycle to have Mickey Thompson taken out." She knew that Goodwin disliked Mickey but didn't realize that he hated him that much to threaten to kill him.

Scott Herman (pseudonym) worked for two years as a clerk for Goodwin's company, Supercross Inc. He indicated that Goodwin would become enraged if Mickey's name was even mentioned, or if he had conversations with his own attorneys about Mickey's lawsuit. Goodwin had filed for business and personal bankruptcy. Herman remembered one particular occasion when Goodwin said, in no uncertain terms, "I'm going to kill that motherfucker." He was referring to Mickey as being the "motherfucker." Mr. Herman was directly outside Goodwin's office when he heard him talking about Mickey. A few seconds later he heard Goodwin throw something against the wall in a rage.

The civil legal matters weren't going well for Goodwin, and he had lost his appeal regarding the lawsuit. In desperation, Goodwin filed a further appeal to the California Supreme Court. By late 1987, or early 1988, Goodwin had an occasion to visit a good friend, Tom Vitter (pseudonym), in Durango, Colorado. Vitter's stepson, Baron Willet (pseudonym), remembers this visit. Goodwin seemed upset at Mickey Thompson. Since Baron was 17 years old at the time, he was very aware of who Mickey was. He was surprised when Goodwin said, "I will take care of Mickey if I lose the civil suit." He didn't give any details in what he meant by 'taking care' of Mickey, but Willet took it to mean that he would do something very bad to Mickey. This conversation took place two to three months before Willet heard about Mickey's death. What was ironic was when he heard of Mickey's death, it was the very day that Goodwin reappeared at his family's house. At that point, Goodwin acted very different from the way Willet had seen him behave on prior occasions.

Another threat occurred in January 1988, at a dinner party, in which Goodwin and his wife Diane were invited to Bill and Nina Winston's (pseudonym) home. Bill Winston, at the time, was general manager of the San Diego Jack Murphy (Later called the Qualcomm) Stadium. He had business dealings with both Goodwin and Mickey at various times when they had sporting events at the stadium. Mr. Winston remembered that he and Goodwin were having a conversation together in the living room while their wives talked in the kitchen. Mr. Winston had just offered Goodwin a drink and asked Goodwin how things were going, and he said, "Terrible." Then Goodwin went on to say, "That fucking Thompson is killing me. I'm going to take him out."

Goodwin went on berating Mickey in a loud voice that could be heard even in the kitchen. Mr. Winston didn't know exactly how to respond but tried to reason with Goodwin. Mr. Winston told him, "Who wins? No one's going to win. He's dead and you'll be in prison." At that point, Goodwin interrupted and said, "Oh no. They'll never catch me. I'm too smart for that." Mr. Winston didn't know what to make of all this. He was just trying to have a nice social evening and didn't think it would turn into such vile threats. After some time, Goodwin seemed to calm down and stated, "Oh, you know I'm only kidding. I would never do anything like that." Nevertheless, Mr. Winston was very upset at the threats Goodwin had made about Mickey, who he considered an old colleague of his.

In January, shortly before the murders, Goodwin continued to express his dislike for Mickey. As Goodwin was waiting for the Supreme Court decision, he had a Super

Bowl party at his home in Laguna Beach. He invited various members of his family. One of those present was a cousin by the name of Greg Knight (pseudonym). Somehow a conversation came up regarding Mickey Thompson, and Goodwin said that Mickey was trying to get all of his money. Then, out of the blue, Goodwin said, "I'll have him wasted." His cousin didn't think much of the statement until he heard several months later that Mickey Thompson had been murdered. Later, in that summer of 1988, Mr. Knight told Mickey's sister, Colleen Campbell, what he had heard Goodwin say. Mr. Knight had been so surprised by Goodwin's statement that he never forgot it.

Unfortunately for Goodwin, the Supreme Court didn't overturn the appellate decision that supported Mickey's position. Goodwin was at the end of the line, and it seemed that Mickey had been victorious. When things seemed that they couldn't get any worse for Goodwin, they did. As had previously been discussed, in February 1988, Mickey took the judgment and had the Marshal's Office attempt to start seizing any property in Goodwin's name. It was Deputy Marshal John Weller (pseudonym) who was given the task of seizing Goodwin's prized Mercedes. The car was very distinctive with the body lowered and all the custom work that had been done on it. At the time, Goodwin and his wife were living at their house in Laguna Beach.

The Marshal's Office could only seize the car if it was in open view. When Deputy Weller drove by Goodwin's house, there was no car in the driveway, so the deputy just continued to drive on to serve papers on other parties. After he had finished, the deputy thought he would try one more time to see if Goodwin's Mercedes might be in the driveway. On his return to the office, Deputy Weller drove back by and saw the glitzy Mercedes parked in the driveway with no one around. Immediately, the deputy pulled in behind the car to block it so no one could drive it away. He placed a yellow sticker on the car officially indicating that it had been seized by the Marshal. Then the deputy called the dispatcher to have a tow truck come to the location and transport the car to a storage yard.

In order to give formal notice, he went to the front door and knocked. Shortly, Goodwin and his wife came to the door. The deputy told Goodwin that his car had been seized and he handed him the court papers. Goodwin told the deputy, in no uncertain terms, that he wasn't taking his car. The situation erupted into yelling and shouting, with Goodwin flying into orbit as he viewed his prized car being hooked to an old dilapidated tow truck. By that time, Goodwin realized there was nothing he could do. The neighbors heard all the noise and began peering outside to see what all the commotion was about. At that moment, Goodwin felt humiliated and powerless. All he could do was lash out at the person who had caused him so much shame and embarrassment.

He told Deputy John Weller that "Mickey is fucking dead. He doesn't know who he's fucking with." Goodwin kept spouting off his dislike for Mickey. This continued even after his car had been towed away. The only consolation was that Deputy Marshal permitted Goodwin to take his personal belongings out of the car. Deputy Weller thought this expression of hatred was more than mere anger, so he started writing down the remarks Goodwin was making. When Deputy Weller returned to his office, he called Mickey's attorney to inform him that they had been successful in seizing Goodwin's car, and he also informed the attorney about the threats that

Goodwin had made against Mickey. It was only a few weeks later that Mickey and Trudy Thompson lay dead on the driveway of their Bradbury home.

CHAPTER 25. ORANGE COUNTY'S INVOLVEMENT

Det. Lillienfeld was assigned the Mickey Thompson case around 1998. At that time, Goodwin was still in federal prison. This made it easy to keep track of his whereabouts. Later, when he was released on parole, he returned to the Southern California area, where he took up residency with his father in an Orange County mobile home park.

After Goodwin's return to Southern California, around 1999, he went to the Gates Boys Gun Store in Orange County and talked to Randy Gibson (pseudonym), the owner. He asked him if there was any way a stun gun could be traced back to a purchaser. Mr. Gibson told Goodwin that some stun guns had serial numbers and others didn't. However, whether there were serial numbers or not, the government didn't require a store to keep records as to the purchasers of stun guns. The basic reason was that a stun gun wasn't considered a device that fired projectiles. Det. Lillienfeld learned about Goodwin's visit to the gun store. When he talked to the owner, he learned that the owner thought it was a strange question to ask. Furthermore, Mr. Gibson wasn't sure if his store had sold a stun gun to Michael Goodwin back in the 1980s. He indicated that his company **may have** sold a stun gun similar to the one recovered at the crime scene, but couldn't be sure.

The stun gun inquiry didn't provide any smoking gun evidence, but it did seem to be a strange inquiry. Sgt. Lillienfeld had learned that Katherine Wilton had been an employee of Goodwin's Motocross Company. When she first started working at the office, she was a secretary in the sales department. In January of 1986, Michael Goodwin had asked her if she would be willing to house-sit their Laguna Beach home while he and his wife Diane went on a ten-day trip. The employee agreed to take care of the house and the dog. While Katherine was at the house, she was looking for a brush to groom the dog. She looked in a cupboard and found a box and saw a handle that she thought might be a brush. When she picked it up, she discovered it was a stun gun. She thought that it was strange and placed it back in the box she had found it in.

The trail of evidence related to the stun gun was interesting, but did it prove anything? All the detectives had was a house sitter who possibly saw a stun gun years earlier and there was no way to say that it was the same type or the same one found at the crime scene. However, these facts provided a so-called nexus to Orange County, where a stun gun was possessed by Goodwin, and the distant possibility that it might have been purchased from the Gibson Boys Gun store in Costa Mesa (which is in Orange County).

The guns that were used to shoot Mickey and Trudy were both 9mm guns. Information became available that indicated Goodwin had purchased two 9mm handguns. Apparently, they were to replace two 9mms that Goodwin had previously purchased years earlier. The investigators surmised that Goodwin had the killers use his two 9mm handguns and had them disposed of after the shooting, and then

Goodwin replaced them with new ones. The only thing that could be proven was the fact that Goodwin had purchased two 9mm handguns from Gibson Boys Gun store.

Det. Lillienfeld had learned from firearms experts that the 9mm guns that Goodwin purchased from Gibson Boys had the same characteristics as the two weapons used in the shooting. This wasn't based on a ballistic matchup but merely a claim that Goodwin had possessed two 9mm handguns that could have been fired at the Thompsons.

With all the follow-up investigation completed, the next question was, where could the Goodwin case be filed? Was there sufficient nexus to file the case in Orange County? There appeared to be sufficient factors that occurred there. The fact that Goodwin had purchased two 9mm automatics similar to the murder weapons and that he had a similar stun gun, both occurring in Orange County, seemed to be enough. Additionally, there was the fact that Goodwin lived in Laguna Beach, which is a part of Orange County, where it was believed he planned the killings. With these factors, the Orange County District Attorney's Office believed they had a sufficient nexus to file the murder conspiracy charges against Goodwin in Orange County if it was brought to them for filing.

CHAPTER 26. ORANGE COUNTY FILED CHARGES

If and when there was sufficient evidence to file criminal charges, the case would be presented to the county prosecutor where the crimes occurred. Since Mickey and Trudy Thompson were shot and killed in Los Angeles County, the obvious prosecutor to review the case for filing would be the Los Angeles County District Attorney's Office. However, the Los Angeles County Sheriff's Department administration and detectives had had numerous conversations with members of the LADA's Office over the years about the evidence—or lack of it—in the Thompson case.

Everyone was aware of the limited amount of incriminating evidence that had been generated. The Johnses' identification of Goodwin in the lineup was of questionable value. How much weight would jurors put on an identification 13 years after the crime? One could argue it was of limited value while others might give it more weight. At that time, the LADA's Office was being besieged by the media, which continued to say "The Los Angeles County District Attorney's Office couldn't win the big cases." The LADA's Office was smarting from all the criticism it had received after the acquittal of O. J. Simpson. The LADA's Office wasn't anxious to file another publicity case especially one with so little incriminating evidence.

Det. Lillienfeld was astute enough to know that it was going to be a hard sell to convince the Los Angeles District Attorney's Office to file such a convoluted case that was entirely based on circumstantial evidence. He may have received bad vibes from the LADA prosecutors he had been in contact with and realized there was no 'Welcome Mat' waiting for him in Los Angeles County.

Det. Lillienfeld wasn't one who shied away from controversy, but he could see the handwriting on the wall. Mickey's sister, Colleen, wanted the case prosecuted. She strongly believed that Michael Goodwin was responsible for the murders. Colleen Campbell was a strong-willed person who didn't give up without a fight. At the time of Mickey's death, she had hired an attorney by the name of Michael Rackauckas to handle Mickey's estate. Later, he was elected to be the Orange County District Attorney. Obviously, because of his background, he was very familiar with the facts of the murder of the Thompsons.

At some point the question was raised whether the Orange County DA's Office could legally prosecute the case. The law was well established that if there was a conspiracy to commit a crime, such as murder, the matter could be prosecuted anywhere one of the overt acts of conspiracy occurred. In other words, if Orange County prosecutors could establish that Goodwin, or one of the killers, committed an act in Orange County, that would give sufficient jurisdiction in Orange County. This was the crack in the door Det. Lillienfeld needed to get the Orange County DA's Office to file criminal charges against Goodwin for conspiracy to commit murder. As tangential as it may seem, Det. Lillienfeld used the fact that Goodwin had supplied the stun gun from his Orange County house and Goodwin had purchased, in Orange County, two 9mm handguns which were identical to the ones used to shoot the Thompsons. With all of these factors, Orange County could arguably be a venue where the Thompsons' murder case could be filed.

Originally, the Orange County DA's Office took the matter to their Grand Jury to have them subpoena various witnesses to appear. The prominent witness was Diane Goodwin. Was the Grand Jury used as a fact finder or to bring charges against Goodwin? Since all the proceedings are secret, it will never be known. However, after the Grand Jury proceedings, there was no indictment of Goodwin. That meant that the Orange County DA would have to file a complaint and leave it up to a magistrate to see if there was enough evidence to hold Goodwin to answer for the charges.

On December 13, 2001, at 3:30 p.m., Det. Lillienfeld went to Goodwin's father's mobile home to arrest Goodwin. They knocked on the door but Goodwin wouldn't open it, so it had to be forced open. When they got inside, Goodwin was placed under arrest. They noticed the rooms were cluttered with papers and books extending all the way to the ceiling. It had the appearance of being the home of a "Pack Rat."

It had taken all of 13 years for the prosecution of the murder case to begin its arduous way through the criminal justice system. But Goodwin wasn't going to roll over and make the case easy for the prosecutors. First, he attacked the Orange County District Attorney, Rackauckas, for handling the case. Goodwin claimed that it was a conflict of interest for him to prosecute since he had represented the Mickey Thompson's estate. The matter went up to the Appellate Court, and they eventually ruled that there wasn't sufficient evidence provided to prove a conflict of interest. That meant the Orange County prosecutor could continue with the case.

Then the case proceeded to have a preliminary hearing to determine if there was sufficient evidence to hold Goodwin to answer for the murder charges. The Orange County prosecutor decided to present most of the evidence against Goodwin, by way of hearsay, through the testimony of Det. Lillienfeld. Since the detective had personally talked to most of the witnesses, it was easy for him to explain what they would testify to, if they were called to court. This speeds up the preliminary hearing process, but it doesn't give the parties an opportunity to see how well a witness would withstand cross-examination.

CHAPTER 27. ORANGE COUNTY PROCEEDINGS

The preliminary hearing seemed to go well for the prosecution. However, the witness regarding the stun gun couldn't remember if he had sold a stun gun to Goodwin. The stun gun was one of the threads that permitted the case to be filed in Orange County. The same witness testified that he had sold Goodwin two sets of 9mm handguns before and after the murders. Det. Lillienfeld testified that the type of 9mm handguns that Goodwin had purchased were the same model of gun that was used to kill the Thompsons. Neither of the handguns used in the murder was ever recovered, so they hadn't been examined by firearms experts.

Little did anyone realize at the time that this was the Achilles Heel of the Orange County case. After all the evidence had been presented at the preliminary hearing, the judge held the defendant, Goodwin, to answer for trial. Goodwin filed a motion that there was insufficient evidence presented. In particular, Goodwin's attorneys argued that the stun gun was not sufficiently connected to the defendant, since the witness couldn't remember if he had sold a stun gun to Goodwin. The Orange County trial court rejected Goodwin's argument. Goodwin didn't give up, and his attorneys took the matter up to the Appellate Court for a second time. At the same time, Goodwin's attorneys submitted a declaration from a firearms expert that the two 9mm handguns purchased by Goodwin couldn't have been the murder weapons. The

Smith &Wesson Company hadn't used that type of twist and grooves in the models that Goodwin had purchased. It was unheard of for a declaration to be submitted to an Appellate Court at that stage of a proceeding. Yet this case had so many unusual features that it wasn't surprising the Appellate Court would make such an exception to allow this declaration to be considered.

The Sheriff's Department reviewed the information in the declaration, and to their surprise the Defense expert was correct. At that point, it was clear that Det. Lillienfeld was wrong when he had testified the 9mm handguns purchased by Goodwin were of the type that could have been used in the slayings. Det. Lillienfeld didn't try to hide his mistake and immediately admitted he was in error. This point was of little value since there were no handguns to physically examine. Yet, the damage had been done. The Appellate Court ruled against the Orange County District Attorney, finding that there was insufficient evidence of venue in Orange County. The Appellate Court went so far as to say that Orange County had no connection to the murders. They stated the mere fact that Goodwin lived in Orange County didn't mean it could be assumed that he did the planning for the murders there. What was even more unanticipated was the fact that the Orange County DA's Office decided they would not continue to appeal the opinion of the Appellate Court up to the California Supreme Court.

This was a victorious day for Michael Goodwin. The Appellate Court ruled that, under the law, the proper venue for a murder case had to be the county where the underlying crime occurred, or where the bodies were found. In the Goodwin case, the Appellate Court said that the proper venue to file the murder charges would be in Los Angeles County since that was where the killings occurred and the bodies were found. That meant that only the Los Angeles County District Attorney's Office could prosecute the case. If they refused to, then Michael Goodwin would be forever a free man. At that point, Goodwin knew that it was highly unlikely that Los Angeles County would charge him, since for all these years they hadn't decided to file anything against him. It was only a matter of days before the order would come from the Appellate Court to release Goodwin from jail.

CHAPTER 28. LOS ANGELES COUNTY DA DECISION

Myths sometimes take on their own life. The news media continually reported that the Los Angeles DA's Office had officially rejected the Goodwin case. This statement was not true, even though the media had made several inferences which were not based on fact. The usual procedure for filing a complaint in the DA's Office is when a law enforcement investigator brings all the paperwork to the DA's Office. There a filing prosecutor reviews all the material. A regular case may consist of a crime report, arrest report, and evidence report, which are reviewed by the prosecutor, and if there is sufficient evidence, then the DA prepares a complaint which he or she signs and the paperwork is taken to the court clerk's office for a filing of the complaint with the court.

However, if the filing deputy believes there isn't sufficient evidence, then he or she will file a formal rejection explaining the reasons, and then it is filed with the DA's Office records unit. Most cases are handled in this way, except special cases that are either complex or publicity cases. Sometimes the law enforcement agency recognizes that the case may need additional investigation. They can ask for a meeting with an appropriate supervisor. There the evidence that exists is discussed, and the investigators may ask what other evidence would be necessary to get a filing for a felony complaint. In those situations, there isn't a formal rejection but a listing of items that would be needed to be done in order to obtain a filing.

In the Goodwin case, the Defense continued to claim that the LADA had formally rejected the case for the reason that there was insufficient evidence. However, there was no formal rejection of the case. Years earlier, the case had been discussed with then-DA Gil Garcetti, and members of his staff. It is unknown what was discussed, but it was clear they didn't think there was enough evidence to file charges against Goodwin. Complex cases, like the Goodwin case, certainly lend themselves to some degree of a subjective assessment. Undoubtedly, the Sheriff's Department may have disagreed with the DA's decision. That may have been the reason they took the matter to the Orange County District Attorney's Office to get a different outcome. But there was never any formal rejection by the LADA's Office.

By 2004, things were changing in the Los Angeles County DA's Office. Steve Cooley was the District Attorney, and he told his staff to take a fresh look at the facts of the Goodwin case to see if there was enough evidence to justify a filing of charges in Los Angeles County. The Goodwin case was like no other. DA Steve Cooley received a highly unusual letter from Goodwin's attorney, which informed him of misstatements that had been made by Det. Lillienfeld. The attorney requested certain items be reviewed before filing any such case against Goodwin. He spelled out his three areas of concern.

First was the fact that Det. Lillienfeld stated that Goodwin had purchased two 9mm handguns before 1984, and again ten days after the shooting he purchased another two 9mm Smith & Wesson which the detective said were consistent with the type of 9mm handguns used in the killing of the Thompsons. Second was Det.

Lillienfeld's claim that Mr. Gibson, the proprietor of Gibson Boys (Sporting Goods Store) had sold a stun gun to Goodwin that was similar to the type of stun gun found on the Thompsons' driveway. Third was Det. Lillienfeld's claim that Mr. Johns positively identified Goodwin's photo as the person parked next to his place two days before the shooting.

The Defense attorney provided specific details illustrating that Det. Lillienfeld was incorrect and fabricated the evidence because he had a vendetta to get Mr. Goodwin. The intent of the letter was clearly to have the LADA's Office disregard the above evidence and to question all the other evidence Det. Lillienfeld might present in regards to filing charges against Goodwin.

It became readily apparent that the Goodwin case evoked considerable consternation. Within the LADA's office, there were mixed opinions about filing or not filing the Goodwin case. The easiest way to resolve the dilemma was to leave it up to the elected DA, Steve Cooley, to make the decision whether to file or not. As a result, the DA decided to have a meeting with his administrative staff and listen to a presentation reviewing all the evidence. The DA wanted all the questions raised by the defense attorney in his letter to be addressed in the presentation. Pat Dixon, the head deputy of Major Crimes Division, was designated as the person to make the presentation.

Pat realized the presentation had to utilize a PowerPoint slide show since that was the most effective way to provide all available evidence for consideration. It was known the District Attorney had a busy schedule, and there were so many issues that needed to be discussed. The question was how to have a full discussion of all the issues in the allotted time. Since Goodwin's release could come in days, it was imperative that the DA make an immediate decision on the issue as to whether or not to file charges. Generally, Pat utilized the services of the Trial Support Division to assist him in preparing the PowerPoint slide show. Since I, Ronald Bowers, (the author) had retired, I was working for the LADA's Office as a consultant on jury trial presentations. So Pat asked me to help him create a PowerPoint presentation.

Some 30 years earlier, Pat had worked for me as a new prosecutor when I was in charge of the West Covina DA's Office. Even then, Pat had a quality of always trying to do the best job possible. He was very intent in whatever he did. Even early on in his career, he had the makings of an extraordinary litigator. On the weekends, Pat worked as a County Life Guard even when he was working for the DA's Office. The job of lifeguarding teaches one to make life-and-death decisions without hesitation. Although it has all the benefits of working on the beach, it still requires one to instill trust and authority among hundreds of beach goers. These are some of the traits that made him an outstanding litigator. He also had one of the most remarkable careers in the DA's Office. He was elevated to Head Deputy of the Major Crimes Division, which required him to oversee the prosecution of the high-powered cases. However, while holding that position, he continued to try additional complex cases that required his special attention.

Since I knew Pat quite well, I had a good idea of what he would want incorporated in his presentation to the DA and staff members. Through Det. Lillienfeld, I obtained all the necessary material I needed to start work on creating a PowerPoint presentation that was complete and visual enough to retain everyone's interest.

After familiarizing myself with all the facts, I met with Pat to find out what he wanted to concentrate on in his presentation to the DA. He wanted a short summary about the attackers carrying out the executions of Mickey and Trudy in their driveway and how these shooters escaped on bicycles. The main part of the presentation was to highlight Goodwin's role in planning and carrying out the murders. Since there was no direct evidence, we had to discuss the threats Goodwin had made to others about harming Mickey.

It was important to spell out Goodwin's motive to harm Mickey and all the events that created all the ill will. To explain this, it was necessary to discuss how Mickey had totally destroyed Goodwin financially by forcing him to declare business and personal bankruptcy. In addition, Pat wanted to focus on what was called evidence of 'Consciousness of Guilt,' which involved the flight after the crime. This included all the evidence showing that Goodwin left the country to live on a yacht somewhere in the Caribbean. In order to prove this, he had to show that Goodwin and his wife sold their property and transferred money to offshore bank accounts.

In less than a week, the big meeting occurred in the DA's Granite Conference room. This name was given to a smaller conference room adjacent to the District Attorney's suite of offices. The reason for this strange name was the fact that the prior DA, Gil Garcetti, had installed a Granite table with the huge seal of the DA's Office inlaid in the center. To some visitors, it might appear somewhat glitzy for a government conference room, which usually appears bland and without frills. However, private law firms have elegant and very stylish conference rooms which, of course, are many times more expensive and are meant to impress potential clients.

The time for the meeting was 2:00 p.m., and I had all the equipment tested beforehand to assure there would be no glitches. The DA administrative staff wandered in and took their usual seats. The DA, Steve Cooley, was still in his office next door conversing on his phone. Pat was pacing back and forth in the conference room. In his hand was a printout of the PowerPoint presentation that he was looking over. As time went by, several of the administrators left the conference room and returned to their offices to carry on their own business.

Around 2:20 p.m., DA Cooley strolled into the conference room and said, "Are we ready?" Seeing the room half empty he said, "Let me know when everyone is here." Then he ambled back to his office and disappeared. One of the administrators followed him to his office. Cooley's secretary, Cathy Musich, phoned the ones who were missing and within moments everyone had reassembled. Cathy walked to Cooley's door and announced everyone was present for the meeting.

Cooley tersely said, "Tell them I will be there as soon as I make this phone call." This was a typical afternoon in the 'front office' of the largest DA's Office in the country. There is constant turmoil occurring that require immediate attention. Some of the daily problems are caused by bizarre rulings by judges. Occasionally police chiefs are dissatisfied with a prosecutor's decision. Even politicians may be seeking vigorous prosecution for certain crimes occurring in their community. Meetings never started on time. Such gatherings only occurred when there was a lull in the storm of the daily crises. It wasn't until 3:15 p.m. when the actual meeting to decide Michael Goodwin's fate began with all the relevant administrators. Pat started his presentation by giving a short history of the recent legal decision of the Appellate Court, which ruled that only the LADA's Office could file charges in this case. This clearly set the tone for the meeting, making everyone aware that Goodwin was going to be set free, depending on the outcome of this meeting.

At that point, Pat moved into the first part of the slide presentation that was related to the description of the crime scene and what evidence was found there. Next, he discussed the neighbor witnesses as to what they had seen, plus the two women in their cars who saw the shooters riding their bikes. Pat was sailing through the facts of what happened on the day of the crime. Everyone was quiet until the issue of the Johnses' identification, which occurred13 years after they claimed to have seen Goodwin scoping out the area two days before the murders. At that point, Pat was inundated with questions, and it seemed as if he was all of sudden in a defensive mode. He could see the momentum fading and was afraid he was never going to be able to cover all the remaining issues.

Pat realized that he had only a limited amount of time before the boss's interest span would be exhausted. To avoid this, he immediately shifted the discussion to Goodwin's threats to harm Mickey. Instantly the questions ceased. He spent several minutes enumerating more than a dozen statements of Goodwin claiming he was going to 'Waste Mickey.' Then Pat made the transition to discussing the evidence pertaining to the 'Consciousness of Guilt' by showing how Goodwin had transferred his assets to offshore banks right after the shooting. This generated questions as to how all this could be proven in court. Pat was prepared with his slides to show how it all could be established by specific witnesses.

District Attorney Cooley sat at the end of the Granite table listening to the questions and answers. Probing questions were asked that illustrated the concern that some of the administrators had regarding such an old case—one which totally relied on circumstantial evidence to show Goodwin's involvement. Cooley had an abbreviated interest span, and after an hour's presentation with discussion, he was ready to move on. He realized that this particular case could be debated forever, in fact it had been discussed for almost 13 years.

Finally, the DA took control of the meeting as everyone realized the 'discussion period' was over. He said to Pat, "Is this a case that can be won in court?" Pat hesitated for a moment, then he tried to summarize the problems with the case. The DA asked again, "Can this Office win this case in court?" Then Pat said in a confident, firm voice that he would personally be willing to try the case. Pat was a high-level supervisor who oversaw the prosecution of the big cases in the DA's Office. It would be most difficult for him to take on such a huge case while being a supervisor. However, he was willing to step up to the plate and actually take on such a difficult challenge.

Cooley paused, seemingly reflecting on Pat's offer to try the case. Cooley pushed back his chair and stood up saying, "Well, if you think there is enough evidence, then file it." He turned and paced back to his office, where he started returning phone calls. Everyone in the conference room sat for a few seconds in silence. Then the room erupted in somber talk about what needed to be done and who should be contacted about the decision to file murder charges against Goodwin.

What was interesting was that Pat never answered the DA's question whether he thought the case could be won. Possibly Pat realized that for the sake of justice some cases just have to be tried. Mickey and Trudy Thompson and their families deserved their day in court. Some cases are so complex and intricate there is no realistic way to predict their outcome. Sometimes the District Attorney has to roll the dice and take a chance. In this case, District Attorney Steve Cooley took a big chance that could ultimately be political suicide for him.

(This graphics page shows how the Goodwin case ended up in the Los Angeles County DA's Office where your author prepared the presentation of the facts and the law that was discussed by the DA administrators headed up by District Attorney Steve Cooley.)

Graphic 16

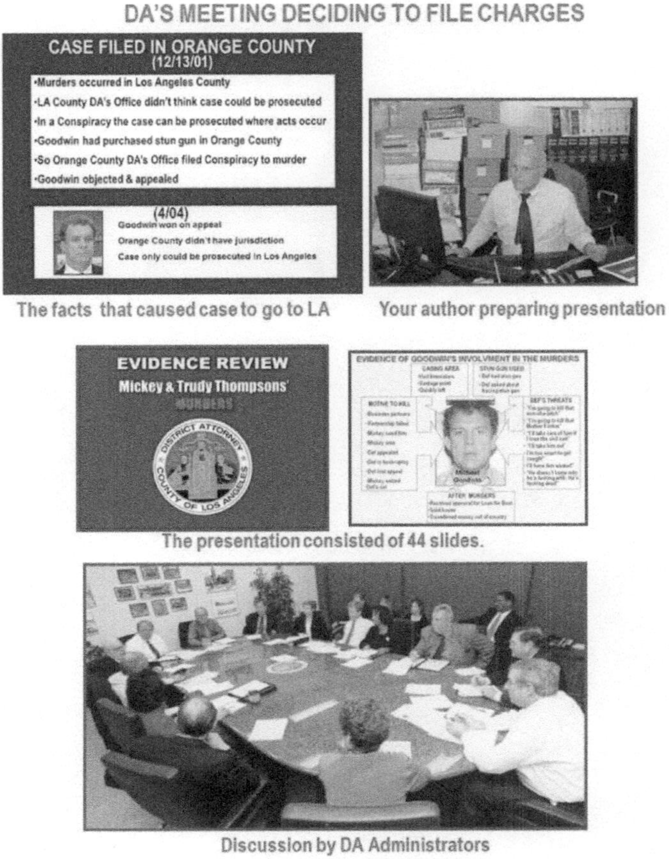

CHAPTER 29. LADA'S OFFICE STRATEGY

Many people were surprised when the LA DA's Office filed double murder charges against Goodwin. Undoubtedly, Goodwin, who was 59 years old when the charges were filed, most likely was the most flabbergasted since the LA DA hadn't filed charges against him during a 16-year period. Finally the LADA filed formal charges on June 8, 2004, and it was Det. Lillienfeld who arrested him in the Orange County jail and then transported him to Los Angeles Main County Jail, where he was booked. Goodwin had been able for all those years to hire private attorneys to defend him every step of the way. However, his money had dried up, and he couldn't find any employment, especially after being convicted on federal fraud charges.

On June 29th, Goodwin was arraigned in the Los Angeles Superior Court branch court in Pasadena. He was asked if he could afford an attorney, to which he responded that he could not. Therefore, a public defender was appointed to represent him. Years earlier, when Goodwin was able to pay his attorneys, he liked to control them by telling them what he wanted them to do. However, when he was given a female public defender, Elena Saris, there was a period of adjustment since he was no longer paying his attorney, so dictating to her what to do was no longer an option. He spent time convincing her that he was an innocent man who was misunderstood. He provided her with stacks of notes and documents that could prove that the cops had the wrong man. As a matter of fact, he claimed the Sheriff's detectives were out to get him. He complained Det. Lillienfeld had a personal vendetta against him and that the detective was working under the direction of Colleen Campbell, Mickey's sister.

The deputy public defender made a motion for bail to be set. Up to that point, Goodwin had always been held without bail. Goodwin indicated he wanted to get out on bail so he could hug his 91-year-old father, who had lost his trailer space in the mobile home park. The deputy DA didn't address the question of Goodwin's family reunion with his dad, but argued to the court that Goodwin was a proven flight risk since he had taken off for two years right after the murders. The judge agreed, and Goodwin remained in custody. Afterward, the media asked Pat Dixon, the lead prosecutor, why the DA's Office was prosecuting someone, when for 16 years they thought there wasn't sufficient evidence against that person. Pat, who had been around the media for many years, realized the media was merely trying to get an emotional reaction from him. He turned to a reporter and in a soft, firm voice said, "We don't file charges unless we believe a reasonable jury will convict." Then he picked up his files and walked away. The reporter looked disappointed in that she didn't get a controversial response.

While Goodwin was held in the Orange County jail, Goodwin continually called reporters up, giving them quotes about his case. He would give interviews to any reporter who was willing to listen. It seemed peculiar for a man who refused for 16 years to talk to the detectives. Nonetheless, he was more than happy to talk to the media and give them his spin on his case. Goodwin had been a media darling in

Orange County; however, things were changing. In Los Angeles County, things would be different.

As a result, the criminal proceedings took on a personal character in that Goodwin wanted to prove that people were out to get him. He didn't seem to focus on trying to prove his innocence but instead maintained that he was a victim of persecution. The prosecution had two battles: one was proving Goodwin was involved in his ex-partners death, and the second was trying to shift attention from Goodwin's sideshow of his hatred toward Det. Lillienfeld and Colleen Campbell. The LADA's Office had to come up with a strategy to deflect the attacks involving Det. Lillienfeld. The best approach was to factor him out by **not** calling him as a witness at trial. Without a doubt this required considerable work locating witnesses who could testify to what Det. Lillienfeld was slated to say in court. Yet it was time well spent since it made for a less contentious case without the sideshow the Defense wanted to present in order to distract the jurors.

Another attack came from the Defense, claiming the prosecution team had viewed privileged documents that had been seized by the Sheriff's Department during Goodwin's arrest and the execution of a search warrant of his father's mobile home where Goodwin lived. The court made a ruling that some of the material might have been privileged and the prosecutors shouldn't have looked at those documents. This became a personal fight since Goodwin's public defender accused prosecutors Pat Dixon and Alan Jackson of having looked at the privileged documents. She argued that they had to be removed from the case because of what they may have seen. As a matter of fact, she even went one step further by claiming the entire Los Angeles County District Attorney's Office had to be removed from the case.

The Defense was hoping to get the case turned over to the State Attorney General's Office. The judge could see where this was all going and eventually Goodwin would claim no one could prosecute the case. At that point, the judge ordered Pat Dixon and Alan Jackson not to look at any of the privileged documents. One wonders what was in those boxes that Goodwin didn't want the prosecutors to see. The judge ordered that a Special Master (an independent attorney) take over custody of the documents and seal any documents deemed privileged. This turned out to be much to do about nothing, but it put another 'fly in the ointment.'

What the prosecution had to concentrate on was the evidence that Goodwin was the person behind the murders. The strongest evidence was **'Motive'**—to get even with Mickey for winning all the civil lawsuits. This demonstrated Goodwin's hatred for Mickey. The prosecution had to find which one of the witnesses still would be able to testify to the threats made by Goodwin. After that, the DA had to spell out what evidence showed 'Consciousness of Guilt,' such as Goodwin's 'Flight' from the area shortly after the murders. The prosecution knew they had some issues to overcome, such as a slight time delay before Goodwin actually left the Southern California area. The LADA's Office had a clear strategic plan how to approach the case, and it was time to dot the 'i's' and cross the 't's.' The prosecutors recognized they had to be ready on every issue that was going to require PREPARATION and then even more PREPARATION.

CHAPTER 30. PRELIMINARY HEARING

Four months after LADA's Office filed charges against Goodwin, a Preliminary Hearing was commenced on Monday, October 4, 2004, in Judge Teri Schwartz's court in Pasadena, California. The purpose of the Preliminary Hearing is to have a magistrate, who is a judge, listen to the prosecution evidence to see if there is sufficient evidence to have the defendant held to answer on the charges. This can be done by having the investigating officer testify to what other witnesses have told him. This is called a "Proposition 115 Prelim." The advantage to this type of hearing is that it speeds up the process. However, the disadvantage for the Defense is that they don't have a chance to cross-examine the original witnesses. But likewise, it doesn't give the prosecutor a chance to evaluate how well the witnesses would do at trial.

The prosecutor, Pat Dixon, called the People's first witness, Gregory Knight, who was a cousin of Goodwin. He testified that he heard Goodwin make threats against Mickey at a family gathering at Goodwin's house in Laguna Beach after the Super

Bowl in 1988. Goodwin appeared angry when Mickey's name was mentioned about their soured business relationship. He further stated, "Before Mickey Thompson gets all of my money I will have Mickey wasted."

The witness said that he didn't think much about the threat. But when he learned about the murder of Mickey, then he believed that Goodwin had something to do with it. He said he was so concerned that he called Colleen Campbell and told her about the threat Goodwin had made. When questioned how well he remembered Goodwin making the statement, he said that he would never forget what Goodwin had said about wasting Mickey.

The next witness was Stu Letterman who was the one who drove Goodwin and Jeannie Sweeney from Laguna Beach to Mickey's attorney's office in Los Angeles. He related how Goodwin went on for 45 minutes explaining how he was going to rip Mickey off. He indicated that he had waited for this opportunity to take advantage of Mickey. After they had arrived back at the office, Goodwin said, "Stu, if you say one word about this, I'll kill you."

The two prosecutors had prepared the questions for all the various witnesses. Then it was time for Alan Jackson to question the next witness, Philip Bartenetti, who had been the attorney and a close friend of the Thompsons. The initial questions were regarding who Mickey Thompson was, other than from common knowledge that he held many speed and endurance records. Then the questions shifted to Mickey's various business ventures, in particular the stadium racing events. Bartenetti was highly knowledgeable about the business deals because he was the one who had drafted the partnership agreement. He explained how the partnership had dissolved and ended in a bitter lawsuit. He also told the court how the 'cat and mouse' game began with Goodwin trying everything he could to prevent Mickey from collecting on the judgment. He outlined how Mickey had won every step of the way. He provided some personal insights by explaining how Mickey didn't like losing at anything, even in athletics. As to Trudy, Bartenetti explained how Mickey totally relied on her when it came to reviewing agreements and contracts. He always gave them to her to evaluate. In essence, Trudy was Mickey's eyes and ears for business decisions.

The next witness was Delores Cordell, an attorney in Bartenetti's firm, who did the Judgment Debtor Exam of Goodwin and his wife, Diane. Delores' testimony was an extension of what Bartenetti had previously testified to. This witness explained the struggle in trying to locate any useful assets to seize to pay off the judgment. The Goodwins had commingled their assets, making it impossible to find anything to take. The bankruptcy court had control over his stadium business. All this attorney could find to levy on was a worn-out engine and an old Mercedes with the license plate of '2 HEAVY.' This witness stated that in her 25 years of handling lawsuits, this without a doubt was the bitterest and most contested.

Other witnesses were called and provided a glimpse into the animosity between Goodwin and Mickey. This included people who had heard Goodwin threaten to harm or kill Mickey. Their testimony was relatively short, basically recalling what Goodwin had said, as well as where and when these threats occurred. The next set of witnesses involved the neighbors who heard and saw part of the shooting of the Thompsons. The first witness on that day was Dr. Jordan, who explained he was awakened by the gunshots. He explained his reaction and that he shot at the shooters as they were escaping. Next witness up was Allison Triarsi, who explained what she saw regarding Mickey having to watch his wife being executed in front of him. There was considerable cross-examination as to how well she remembered something that occurred so many years earlier.

Sgt. Verdugo laid out the crime scene and where the various pieces of evidence were found. His testimony was most foundational and didn't elicit much in the way of cross-examination. Following him was witness Liz Devine, who explained her role in locating evidence, as well as her memory as to what happened to the orange peels that were seen near Mickey's body.

October 11, 2004, was Columbus Day, which was a court holiday. It always seemed strange that the court would take this day off, since certain groups have been quite critical of Christopher Columbus for his relationship with the American Indians. But the courts aren't willing to give up this holiday even though Columbus is presently out of favor with certain groups. So after the holiday break, the court resumed the prelim on Tuesday. The prosecutors saved the more controversial witnesses for the end of the preliminary hearing. Mr. and Mrs. Johns were called as witnesses. Mr. Johns testified first and explained that he came home around 11:00 a.m. and noticed a car parked next to his property on the wrong side of the road. He asked his wife how long they had been there. He noticed that the driver had binoculars and he was looking in the direction of the elementary school. As he approached the car he could see that it was an old Malibu Chevrolet station wagon that was highly oxidized. As he got closer, he could see that the driver was a white male who had a black watch cap on. He had reddish hair and his face had a ruddy complexion and was pockmarked.

Ron Johns related that he was able to get within eight feet when the man looked at him and immediately started the car and drove off. Ron's wife was right behind him when the station wagon drove off. He didn't think much about it until several days later when he heard about the murders. He mentioned what he had seen to deputies, who didn't think it sounded relevant. It wasn't until 13 years later that the Sheriff's detectives contacted him. Then the prosecutor asked Mr. Johns if he could identify the driver and he pointed to the defendant in the courtroom.

Tonya Johns testified similarly to her husband regarding when her husband pulled up and asked about the car. He walked over to the car, and she followed. She could see a white man in the driver's seat. As they got closer to the fence, the man looked at them and quickly left. She was asked if she could identify the driver and she indicated she could, and it was the defendant who was seated at the counsel table.

The Defense attorney, Elena Saris, did extensive cross-examination of both the Johnses. She was trying to pin them down on how they could identify a person they saw over 13 years ago. The Johnses remained firm in their identifications. However, the next witness was the person on the top of the Defense's list to thoroughly cross-examine. That person was Gail Humphrey (pseudonym) who was the witness who could put the final nail in the defendant's coffin. She was the witness who provided the prosecution with a confession to the murders.

Deputy DA Alan Jackson asked Gail if she knew the defendant and she indicated she did. When asked where she had met Goodwin she indicated that she met him at a ski lounge and he gave her his business card. She became impressed with him, and they started living together at the end of 1990 up until late in 1992. She remembered one morning he burst into the master bedroom with a VHS tape in his hand and put it in the VCR and started playing it. It was a recording of the TV program Unsolved Mysteries and was a re-enactment of the Thompsons' murders.

What surprised her was when he said, "Look what I've done and I got away with it." From that point on he couldn't stop talking about Mickey Thompson." She was shocked but didn't tell anyone because he always had a gun next to the bed and he had threatened her with it if she ever told on him or left him. Goodwin went on to say, "Mickey was so predictable as to what he did every morning."

The Defense attorney waited patiently for the prosecutor to finish his questioning of Gail. Then the Defense let loose and asked her about her medical condition and why she was placed in a medical facility. She claimed that Goodwin had beaten her and that was the reason for the hospitalization. She admitted that she had been treated as an alcoholic. Defense counsel Elena Saris did a classic job attacking this witness in showing the court how much she disliked the defendant and how her statements varied from being beaten by the defendant to her attempt to commit suicide.

By the time the Defense attorney had finished with this witness, the two prosecutors were looking at each other shaking their heads. Both prosecutors had to wonder if it had been worth using such an incriminating confession at the price of all the baggage that this witness brought to the witness stand. How would the jurors judge her? Would they believe her or consider her a vindictive person who would do anything to hurt the person who had hurt her?

Even putting aside the value of this last witness, the judge had to make a ruling. After listening to all the evidence, Judge Teri Schwartz said, "There's simply no one else the court can say committed this crime." Then the judge went on to say, "The court has no problem in finding enough evidence to connect this defendant to these crimes." She formally held Goodwin to answer on the charges and continued to issue a no bail ruling.

CHAPTER 31. CHECKING OUT CRIME SCENE

Crime Scenes change over time, especially after 18 years, so the prosecution needed to know what those changes were and how they might affect a jury viewing of the crime scene. Also, the prosecutors needed to see first-hand the scope of the crime scene. The DA's Office decided on a personal visit to the Thompson's address to check out the driveway and the layout of the neighborhood. There were issues as to whether the Triarsi witnesses could actually see the shooting from their house. Alan Jackson arranged for Mark Lillienfeld to bring along retired Sgt. Ray Verdugo, who had been at the Thompson house on the morning of the shooting. Everyone met at the base of the old Thompson house at 1:00 p.m. Obviously, the Thompsons no longer lived there and, as a matter of fact, the property had been sold to various owners over the years.

Old crime scene photos were removed from a tattered folder. The group of prosecutors and detectives started to flip through them. In order to stage a quasi-re-enactment, the group wanted to review exactly where the bodies were located on the driveway. After gazing at the photos of Trudy's body at the bottom of the driveway, they meticulously laid down a sheet. It represented the spot where Trudy's body was lying in the street gutter below the driveway. Then it was decided to proceed to the top of the driveway and place a sheet where Mickey's body was lying. In this way, it could be determined if Mickey could actually view where Trudy was shot. This would be crucial to the prosecution's theory of the case.

They spent several minutes trying to line up the top sheet to correspond to the old crime scene photos of Mickey lying on the driveway. The detectives looked up at the old Thompson house and saw several children with their faces pressed against the window panes staring out at the sheets in the driveway. Det. Lillienfeld strolled over to the front door to find the new owners and inform them about the re-enactment. The children scurried around inside the house loudly asking for an adult.

Shortly thereafter a young lady came to the door. It wasn't clear if she was the mother, a housekeeper, or babysitter. She had a blank stare on her face. Det. Lillienfeld in his folksy, down-home voice explained he was from the Sheriff's Department and they were there to view the driveway. The lady didn't have any objection and seemed more concerned that the children were quarreling. The detectives didn't know how much to tell her. They mentioned that this used to be the Thompsons' house. With a shrug of her shoulder, her reaction seemed to say, who are the Thompsons? Then the detectives wondered if the sellers of the property ever told the new buyers that the driveway of their newly purchased house had been the crime scene for one of the biggest unsolved double murders of all times.

The detective didn't want to frighten the lady, so he didn't go into any details about the homicides but merely asked if they could walk around the front of the house for a few minutes. By then the woman was holding a small child and she nodded OK as though she didn't care. The detectives thanked her, and she closed the door and disappeared somewhere in the huge Thompson house.

The detective rejoined the prosecutors, who were standing next to a sheet where Mickey's body had been located. They were trying to check to see if the crime scene evidence supported the belief that one of the shooters was in the bushes before the attack. Ray Verdugo said he remembered that there were several bullet holes in the garage door. Everyone started looking closely at the garage door for any type of holes. The challenge was who would be the first to find one. Verdugo said, "Here's one of the bullet holes." Then a little bit higher was another bullet hole. Even after all those years, the bullet holes were still visible. Since they were so small, no one found it necessary to fill them in with putty or dowels. These bullet holes totally supported the idea that the shooter shot from the brushy area. Following the trajectory of those shots, the projectiles would strike the garage door right where the bullet holes were found.

Upon resolving that issue, the prosecutors and detectives returned to the bottom of the driveway, where they pulled out more photos showing the neighbor's house. After orientating themselves, they climbed up the neighbor's driveway to the Triarsi house to see if the sheets were viewable from that house. The re-enactment confirmed that the Allison Triarsi, the 14-year-old, could actually see what she claimed she saw.

The next issue to be examined was whether Dr. Jordan could see the bicyclists coming down the back path to the Thompson property. A bicycle was used to reenact how the shooters escaped. From Dr. Jordan's house, he would have been able to see the bicyclists on the bottom area of the path as they converged onto Woodlyn Lane. There would have been some tree branches to block a small portion of his view, but that would have been minuscule to the overall viewing.

The visit to the crime scene having been completed, everyone returned to their vehicles and drove over to the south gate to see if Mrs. Wilma Johnson's statement was accurate that the bicyclists zoomed in front of her car while she was driving eastbound on Royal Oaks Drive. When they arrived at this location there was no traffic. Prosecutor Alan Jackson was able to stand exactly where Mrs. Johnson would have been driving when the bicyclists darted in front of her car. There was no way the bicyclists could have seen her driving eastbound on the street since there was a large block wall obscuring their vision of her. No one could quite visualize how the bicyclists were able to enter the regional bike pathway.

By visiting the escape route, it was clear that a bicycle could squeeze between the break in the fence and could be long gone within minutes. Then the attention was directed to the Johnses' house, where the eyewitnesses claimed they saw Goodwin scoping out the location two days before the shooting. Everyone got back in their cars and drove several blocks to the east of the house. When they arrived, it was confusing where the Johnses were standing when they viewed Goodwin sitting in the old station wagon. Sgt. Verdugo tried to explain the various locations of where everyone had been. Alan stood there, trying to visualize the scene, but kept asking questions. What distances were the Johnses away from seeing Goodwin? Who was in the driver's side of the station wagon?

Then Verdugo said it would be easier to understand the situation if they did a re-enactment. So a Ford Explorer was utilized to pretend to be the station wagon, and Verdugo pulled it up on the wrong side of the street, just the way the Johnses had described it. Verdugo pretended to be Goodwin sitting in the Explorer, and Det. Lillienfeld stood next to the corral fence just where Mr. Johns would have been standing two days before the shooting. The prosecutor stood to the side of Det. Lillienfeld and pretended he was trying to look into the station wagon. Alan exclaimed that he had an unobstructed view of the occupant in the car and could even see a passenger who would have been on the other side of Goodwin.

Everything added up as to what the eyewitnesses had said. The old photos could be used to show where everything took place. After this walk-through, the prosecutors felt comfortable in having a jury view of the various key locations in the City of Bradbury.

(The following graphic page shows investigators and prosecutors reenacting the crime scene locations)

Graphic 17

CRIME SCENE REENACTMENT

Author & Sgt. Verdugo reviewing report

Checking view Mickey had of Trudy

Sgt. Verdugo showing escape route

Examining the Johns' view of Goodwin in car

Investigating South Gate that shooters used to escape

CHAPTER 32. FINALLY THE TRIAL BEGINS

Since the crime occurred in Bradbury, the proper courthouse to handle the case would be the Pasadena Branch of the Superior Court. The courthouse is a tall, sterile concrete building that seems so out of character with the grand architecture of Pasadena. Adjacent to the unattractive courthouse are the City Hall and City Library, with their neo-classic grandeur. In years past, Pasadena was the winter home for the eastern tycoons, who would travel by train to this fair city with its rough-hewn bungalows stretching all the way down Orange Grove Blvd. Today, Pasadena is best known for its renowned New Year's Rose Parade followed by the Rose Bowl football game, which is considered the Granddaddy of all the bowl games.

All the attorneys in the Goodwin case had their offices in downtown Los Angeles in the Criminal Courts Building, making it extremely inconvenient to try the case in an outlying branch court. Although Pasadena would be considered by most as a very diverse community, the Pasadena court jury pool would be made up of 'stakeholders' who generally own their homes and feel attached to their neighborhood. This would give a slight advantage to the prosecution since some of the jurors would have a 'law and order' leaning. Yet, the prosecution was leery of the engineers who were a part of Cal Tech and Jet Propulsion Lab, both located in Pasadena. Prosecutors all have stories how they have had problems with engineers being on a jury. Most engineers are more comfortable when they can add up all the evidence to get an answer. However, the legal concept of 'Reasonable Doubt' doesn't lend itself to a specific black-and-white answer.

By November 6, 2006, at 10:10 a.m. one of the longest-running murder mysteries of all times was about to commence. The Goodwin case was about to begin in a miniature courtroom that was bulging at its seams. Court watchers, reporters, and relatives of the victims had to compete for the few courtroom seats. One could only wonder why the judicial administration wouldn't have thought of using one of their huge courtrooms to try one of the biggest cases assigned to the Pasadena courthouse. One learns not to question judges as to why they don't take into consideration the comfort of the audience. The bailiff called the court to order, and Judge Terri Schwartz entered the packed courtroom and took her place in the tall judge's chair. Although she is of medium height, the oversized chair dwarfed her. She had been a deputy DA for years before becoming a judge, and had developed a good reputation as a solid litigator. As a judge, she had taken on the patient look of not projecting any emotion or expression. She was all business, which isn't a bad trait when you are trying a case in her courtroom.

The judge addressed the courtroom by clarifying some basic rules regarding the trial and explained that parts of the trial would be televised. There were two remote-controlled cameras recording the proceedings, but at no time were they to show the faces or any part of the jurors. At the back wall of the courtroom, a technician was hidden unceremoniously behind a black curtain, where he controlled the cameras and the microphones. The media had tried to adjust to the cozy atmosphere in the tiny courtroom.

The counsel table was congested with four attorneys who were forced to be in each other's personal space. There was no place to hide notes or any confidential reports without the other side seeing what you had. Michael Goodwin was sandwiched between his two defense attorneys. He was dressed in a brown suit with a white shirt and a tie with a design of autumn leaves on it. His appearance was that of a businessman who was consumed with what was going on around him. His full, curly reddish-gray hair framed a middle-aged face that held horn-rim glasses that were propped on his nose. Anxiously, he seemed to be writing in a notebook as though he was about to announce some revelation.

Goodwin's intensity was only upstaged by his lead Public Defender, Elena Saris, who was decked out in a dark suit with her stringy hair going in every direction. She may have purposely tried to do the 'stringy permed look' to project an older image since she was the youngest looking person in the courtroom. Her face was devoid of any hint of a smile. She conveyed a hypersensitive seriousness. Based on her mannerisms to her speech, she was 110 % committed to fighting for her client, Michael Goodwin. The jurors could sense her intensity and commitment to the defendant. However, would the jurors be turned off by her failure to connect with them on a personal level? Only time would tell. She was assisted by another appointed attorney, Tom Summers, who was assigned to handle the business aspect of the Defense case. He rounded out the crowded counsel table, forcing him to sit at the corner end of the table.

As intimate as the courtroom seemed, the prosecutors weren't happy with the configuration of the courtroom. Every time a juror walked in, they would have to pass within one yard of the defendant. Goodwin early on learned to smile at each juror who would walk right next to him. Prosecutors dislike it when jurors have to walk within the personal space of a defendant. Most courtrooms are laid out so that the jurors utilize the side doors of the courtroom. Judge Schwartz's courtroom left so much to be desired. To prevent a mini-friendship from developing between jurors and the defendant, the prosecutors would both stand up as the jurors entered or left the courtroom. This created a diversion, so the jurors weren't looking directly at a smiling Michael Goodwin.

CHAPTER 33. DA'S OPENING STATEMENT

The judge turned to the prosecutors and asked if they wished to make an Opening Statement. Deputy DA Alan Jackson slowly stood up and said, "The People would, Your Honor." Alan could be described as a young, handsome professional. He hailed from Texas and was proud of it but didn't retain any noticeable southern accent. When he was speaking and trying to emphasize a point, he often slipped in one of his "You all" Texas sayings. His mannerisms exuded confidence, and he projected a genuine sincerity. He was never short on ambition and certainly he had a good sense of what was needed to advance his career. His personality would be described as likeable, conveying a respectable image.

He fits in well with the young men in the office because of his interest in sports cars, skiing, and socializing at sporting events. However, everyone learns to avoid discussing college football with him because of his blinding bias for the University of Texas. Young women in the DA's Office seemed to be impressed with his charm, and the older women wanted to adopt him and mother him. The immediate question was, how would he relate to or connect with the jurors he was about to address?

He nodded the pre-arranged signal to the court clerk to turn the lights down in the courtroom so the jurors could better see his PowerPoint presentation. Alan said in his most congenial voice, "Good Morning!" This is a crucial moment for every attorney. The jurors' response will provide insight as to whether they are with you or against you. His boyish smile may have broken the ice, because the jurors roared back in unison a loud "Good Morning."

That was the tone the prosecution needed to start the lengthy process of showing the jurors all the pieces of the puzzle to prove Goodwin was behind the killings of the Thompsons. From that point on, Alan started laying out his case by starting to explain who Mickey Thompson was.

"On September 9, 1960, Mickey Thompson was strapped in his racecar he had built to attempt to set a world speed record for piston-driven vehicles. He revved up his 2800-horsepower engine and headed down the Bonneville Salt Flats. By the time he was clocked at going 406.6 mph which made him the fastest man alive on wheels. From that point on Mickey was known worldwide."

After introducing the jurors to who Mickey Thompson was, he started his next task, which was showing them how Mickey and Michael Goodwin came together to form a partnership. He explained how Mickey wanted to decelerate his business activities because of Trudy's health problems. So Mickey turned to Goodwin, who was in the same business as him, although concentrating more on motorcycle racing. They agreed to a partnership with a split of 30% for Mickey and 70% for Goodwin. The prosecutor explained how this partnership quickly dissolved.

"On March 30th, 1984, they signed the Partnership Agreement. From that very day, Goodwin had 'bad intentions' as to his dealing with Mickey. Goodwin was already figuring on ways to rip off Mickey. However, Goodwin may not have realized who he was dealing with. It all

started to unravel from their first event, which was at Pontiac Stadium when Goodwin didn't put up the money required and Mickey got stuck paying the expenses."

Deputy DA Alan Jackson laid the foundation for the jurors to understand the next step, which was the **'Motive'** factor. He related to the jurors the lawsuit Mickey brought against Goodwin for the $500,000 when Mickey got stuck paying for expenses that Goodwin was obligated to pay. Every step of the way Mickey was successful in winning all the lawsuits against Goodwin. Alan explained Goodwin's reaction to all this losing.

"This became a pattern of losing for Goodwin. He didn't like to lose. Both men had giant egos, so they were going to fight through numerous lawsuits. As the years went by Goodwin continued to lose at every step of the way."

Then the game was on between the two. Mickey wanted to collect on the judgment he had won against Goodwin. However, in spite, Goodwin tried to checkmate Mickey from getting any of his assets. Goodwin went to great lengths to shield his assets. Still, Mickey hired attorneys to track down any real or personal property Goodwin owned. With all this litigation, the prosecutor was trying to paint a picture of Goodwin obsessed with a 'Pattern of Losing' which became the **'Motive'** for wanting to kill Mickey.

The prosecutor wanted the jurors to see the full impact these losses had on Goodwin. So he dramatically listed them on a PowerPoint slide.

PERSONAL LOSSES

- Goodwin lost the civil lawsuit

- Goodwin lost his Mercedes
- Goodwin lost the Insport Agreement
- Goodwin lost the Rose Bowl events
- Goodwin lost the Anaheim events

COURT LOSSES

- Goodwin lost his business (bankruptcy)
- Goodwin lost personal assets (bankruptcy)
- Goodwin lost at the Appeal Court
- Goodwin lost at the Supreme Court
- Goodwin lost counter suit
- Goodwin lost request to discharge his personal debt in bankruptcy

Jackson hammered away at all the losses Goodwin suffered at the hands of Mickey Thompson. During the preparation of this case, the DA's Office realized that as confusing and boring all these legal documents were, it was important for the jurors to understand the pattern of losses in order to prove the **'Motive.'** Next, the prosecutor turned to the threats that Goodwin had made over the years to harm Mickey and his family. Jackson titled this evidence as part of his **Vendetta** to get even with Mickey. In order for the jurors to feel the impact of the threats, he listed them on separate slides of his presentation.

"I'm going to kill that son of a bitch." (referring to Mickey) (Spring 1986)

"You know Mickey, I can have you taken out; have you fixed."(Spring 1986)

"I'm going to kill that mother fucker" (Feb. 1987)

"I'm going to take care of him if I lose the civil suit." (Early 1988)

"Thompson is destroying me. I'm gonna take him out." (Jan. 1988)\

"I hate him. I'd like to kill him." (Jan. 1988)

"The only way I can come out ahead is by taking care of Mickey." (Late 1980)

"You took everything. I'm gonna get it back. I'll kill you." (Late 1980s)

"Mickey doesn't know who he's fucking with. He's fucking dead!" (Feb. 1988)

"Before he sees a dime, I'll have him wasted." (Early 1988)

To dramatize his point, the prosecutor's next slide displayed the words **"March 16, 1988, I'll have him wasted"** and seconds later the photos of the dead bodies of

Mickey and Trudy appeared on the screen. This was a gripping moment when everyone in the courtroom was mesmerized by the combining of the victims with Goodwin's words that he wanted them **"WASTED."** Jackson continued to show the jurors the crime scene and the involvement of the witnesses who corroborated the fact that Mickey had begged the shooters not to kill his wife. Afterward, the shooters had executed Trudy before Mickey's eyes, then shot him in the head.

Since this case was entirely based on circumstantial evidence, the prosecution team knew how important it was for the jurors to comprehend the rivalry between these two men and how Goodwin had expressed his hatred for Mickey. This was the connection that the prosecution needed the jurors to grasp.

After his lengthy Opening Statement, Alan Jackson sat down to a totally quiet courtroom. Within moments the judge broke the silence by saying, "This would be a good place to break for lunch, after which the Defense will have the opportunity to give their Opening Statement."

(The following graphic page shows prosecutor Alan Jackson giving his Opening Statement with his slide show.)

Graphic 18

DA'S PRESENTATION

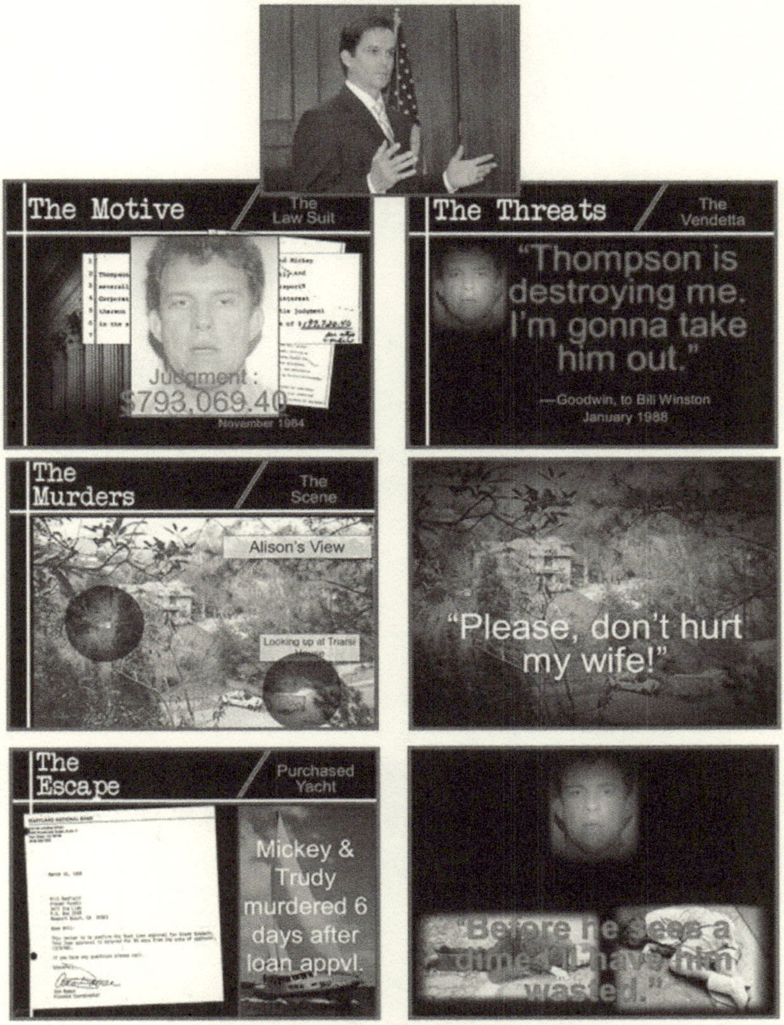

Alan Jackson's PowerPoint Slide Presentation

CHAPTER 34. DEFENSE OPENING STATEMENT

After the noon break, it was time for Goodwin's Public Defender, Elena Saris, to make her Opening Statement. As she rose to the occasion, it was her job to erase from the jurors' memory the image of Mickey and Trudy lying in their own pools of blood with the words "I'll have them wasted." She used her own PowerPoint presentation but concentrated her efforts to directly discuss the case with the jurors. She tried to build a theme for her case by saying the following:

"Keep in mind the 'Naked Suspicion' since the People's case has no clothes on it. The prosecution has never caught the shooters, they have no weapon, there is no forensic evidence, and no evidence to connect Goodwin to the crimes."

There was a slightly puzzled look on the faces of the jurors as to what she meant by a 'Naked Suspicion.' It may have been too sophisticated or the wrong analogy. Her next point was that Hollywood had twisted the story to give it a horrific quality in which Mickey was kept alive in order for him to see his wife executed before his eyes. She indicated that no one at the time of the crime ever said or implied that Mickey had been forced to watch his wife being murdered.

"Unfortunately, this case has gotten some folklore and Hollywood slant that are untrue. The facts of the case have been the subject of many TV programs such as Unsolved Mysteries.

When the case is examined it all falls apart. This was the idea that the gunmen went to great lengths to keep Mickey alive so he could see Trudy being killed."

This was a strange Defense since they were going to use ballistic evidence to prove that Mickey may have been killed first and he wasn't able to see his wife Trudy being killed. Her explanation was as follows:

"The top gunman shot at Mickey three times, as shown by the three expended casings on the ground and that the gunman must have walked down the driveway because there was another extended round halfway down the driveway. Mickey was shot seven times in total, and the idea was to show Critical Mass. It appeared that one shooter was a better hit man because they were spending ***live rounds*** *when they pulled the slide back on the automatic."*

Defense attorney Elena Saris was so intense in the delivery of her presentation that some of the jurors were staring at her with a glare of "I want to believe you but what are you talking about?" At that point, she shifted gears to attack the Sheriff's investigation for not doing something with Trudy's fingernail scrapings. It was unclear what these scrapings had to do with connecting Goodwin to the case, but she wanted the jurors to know that she had them tested, even though the Sheriff hadn't analyzed them. At that point, one wondered whether these ideas expressed in the Opening Statement were being orchestrated by Michael Goodwin, who was expressing his thoughts by using the voice of his defense attorney.

To continue with the theme of 'I am a better investigator than the Sheriff,' defense counsel Saris said that the stun gun found in the driveway had tape on the bottom to hold the batteries in place. She revealed that when the Defense had it analyzed, 18 years later, they found a hair stuck to the tape. To support her claim of having better investigating skills than the Sheriff, she said that the Defense had the single hair tested for DNA and it turned out not to be Goodwin's DNA.

The jurors politely listened, and people in the audience wondered why everything involving Goodwin was a contest in which he was smarter and always the WINNER. Then the Defense went on the attack of what they claimed were the **'Animosity Witnesses.'** Defense attorney Saris seemed to be at her best and took on each of the witnesses that the prosecution claimed had overheard Goodwin making threats against Mickey. She revealed to the jurors that law enforcement, with the help of Mickey's sister, had offered a million-dollar reward for supplying evidence to convict those involved in the two murders. Several male jurors' eyes lit up when she mentioned the money.

She started with Bill Winston (pseudonym), who had claimed Goodwin threatened Mickey when Goodwin and his wife were over at his house for dinner. She claimed Winston revealed the threat only after the reward was offered. Then Saris claimed that he kept changing the date when this incident occurred, in order to make it closer to the time of the murders. Then she targeted John Weller, the Deputy Marshal who repossessed Goodwin's prized Mercedes. Her criticism of his announcement of the threat was the fact that he was somehow mixed up on his dates. Then she added that Goodwin voluntarily gave up his Mercedes because he was about to move on to his new sailboat and wouldn't have any need for his Mercedes.

The defense attorney was getting traction on the threatening statements, and the jurors had noted that they wanted to know more about those prosecution witnesses. Then she got to the strongest point of the defense, and that was the identification by

Mr. and Mrs. Johns of Goodwin casing the location below the Thompson house two days before the shooting. She said the following, which made some of the jurors lean back in their seats and take note:

"The Johnses claimed to be able to identify the defendant as the person outside their house some 14 years later. Mr. Johns said that they hadn't seen anything on TV, but his wife says to the contrary. Mr. Goodwin's photo had been on the TV many times."

She had scored a bullseye with the jurors as to the Johnses' identification 14 years after the shooting. This was where the jurors realized that they were going to have to examine the prosecution's case more carefully because such a late identification certainly could be fraught with problems. Since the Defense counsel was on a roll, she decided to go one step further and prove that the real motive for the killings was a **'robbery gone bad.'** The defendants in American courts don't have to prove anything. In many cases, the defendant doesn't testify and often doesn't present any witnesses, and his or her Defense attorney argues that the prosecution didn't prove its case beyond a 'Reasonable Doubt.'

However, it is risky for the Defense to claim that it is going to prove something because the jurors are going to judge the Defense on whether they proved what they said they would. She said the following, which suggested that they were going to prove it was a robbery-murder:

"The two eyewitnesses who saw two males leaving on bicycles said both had drawstring canvas bags. This was strange that they would have such bags. The prosecution said that there was no evidence of robbery but, in fact, there were shoe prints near a door that goes to

the back of the elevator located in the garage and, in fact, Mickey kept three safes in the garage."

Even though the DA claimed there was no evidence of a motive of robbery, it was unclear what the Defense wanted the jurors to believe. Was the Defense saying it was going to prove the two shooters were somehow attempting to rob the safes in the garage? It seemed that the Defense was throwing things against the wall and seeing what would stick. Finally, Saris concluded her Opening Statement by saying the following:

"It has taken 18 years of investigation including just about every investigative agency. All the prosecution evidence, when examined, only shows a NAKED SUSPICION and that is all."

The Defense attorney shuffled her notes together and returned to her seat and sat down next to her client, who gave her a gigantic smile of approval. Some jurors had a perplexed look as though they had heard enough and wanted time to digest it all. Others had a half smile as though they were glad the beginning was all over and they could get up and stretch.

CHAPTER 35. DA'S EVIDENCE AT TRIAL

The prosecution had created a colossal logistic problem for itself in taking on this case, which relied so heavily on circumstantial evidence. In order to prove Goodwin's guilt, the DA potentially had to call over 70 witnesses. Since the case had occurred over 18 years earlier, many had retired and some had moved out of the area. The prosecutors had to accept the fact that the witnesses wouldn't be called in a coherent order but on the basis of their availability to come to court. Alan Jackson, in his Opening Statement, had warned the jurors that the witnesses would be called out of order, and he tried to explain what category each witness should be grouped in as follows:

1—the **Business** dealings of the partnership and lawsuits;

2—the **Threats** made by Goodwin;

3—the **Crime Scene**;

4—Goodwin **Scoping out the area**;

5—**Consciousness of Guilty** of Goodwin's flight from the area;

6-- Goodwin's **Confession** to the crime.

The first example of witnesses being taken out of order was when William Winston was called as the first witnesses. He would fit in the Second category, involving threats made by Goodwin. William Winston had previously been a Pasadena police commander, and when he retired, he took over as general manager of the Rose Bowl and later moved on to Jack Murphy Stadium in San Diego. He was asked if he had a dinner party in which Goodwin and his wife Diane attended at his house in San Diego. He acknowledged he had. Then he was asked whether there was any conversation about Mickey Thompson. The witness said there was. He related that Goodwin said the following: "He told me that he was miserable because Mickey Thompson was ruining his life. He stated that Mickey had broken him emotionally and financially." He further related that "Thompson is killing me . . . he's destroying me, he's taking everything I've got. I'm going to take him out." When he was told that if he killed Mickey, he would end up in prison, Goodwin replied, "They'll never catch me." Later in the evening, Goodwin cooled down and said he was only kidding.

Throughout the trial, the prosecution called numerous witnesses who related to the jury various threats that Goodwin had made about his hatred of Mickey and how he would waste him. The Defense attorney attacked all these witnesses as either being motivated to obtain part of reward money or as trying to help Mickey's sister. Since these witnesses had told their stories numerous times, she tried to show the witnesses had been inconsistent on the wording of the threats or gave different dates when they occurred. In her cross-examination, she tried to plant a seed of doubt about the threats.

Another early witness called was Elizabeth Devine, who had been the criminalist who responded to the Thompson crime scene for the Sheriff's crime lab. She was one of the witnesses who required special attention because of her tight schedule, not because of her crime lab duties. Over the past 18 years, this witness found herself in great demand because of the popularity of the CSI television programs. Eventually, she left the Sheriff's crime lab to become an associate producer on the CSI production company. Besides making enormous amounts of money in her new position, she had an extremely busy schedule since this was the time for the filming of all the CSI shows.

Therefore, the prosecutor tried to accommodate her schedule by calling her as one of the first witnesses. She testified that when she arrived at the scene, she checked out the entire crime scene, looking for items to be seized and samples to be taken. She noticed pools of blood under the bodies of the victims. A stun gun was pointed out to her on the driveway. There were numerous shell casings scattered all over the driveway, as well as several unexpended bullets. When she was near the top of the driveway, she noticed orange peels under tall brush. She examined the peelings and noticed they were quite fresh. It appeared that someone had picked an orange from the orange tree next to the garage. They had walked a short distance to where they peeled it and threw the peelings on the ground.

The prosecution was using this incident to show that the killers had been lying in wait for Mickey and Trudy to leave for work in the morning. Since the DA's Office had pled the special allegation of 'Lying in Wait,' this was proof that the killers had been waiting some time to commit the murder. However, Goodwin's attorney started asking embarrassing questions as to where were the orange peels and had they been tested for DNA? It was never clear if the orange peels had ever been picked up. There was no record of them being seized. Further, she was asked if she had written a script about the Thompson case and the missing orange peels. She indicated that she had used a similar idea in one of the CSI programs. The Defense had planted the seed that the Sheriff's Department had not done a very thorough job of retaining the potential evidence.

Other witnesses were called about conducting the investigations of the crime scene. Sgt. Ray Verdugo was the main witness who walked the jury through the evidence that was found at the crime scene. The Defense's cross-examination concentrated on what the Sheriff's investigation didn't do or should have done to identify or catch the two shooters who were never arrested or prosecuted.

As to the witnesses who saw or heard parts of the shooting and the escape, their testimony was crucial. This was to support the DA's position that Mickey was kept alive in order to witness his wife being executed. These key witnesses were Allison Triarsi and her father Anthony Triarsi, who lived on the hill across a small valley between the two houses. They both recalled hearing shots and Trudy screaming, "Please don't kill me." At the same time, they heard Mickey say, "Please don't hurt my wife." Then Mr. Triarsi said he saw a man standing over Trudy who turned to look up the driveway where Mickey was on the ground with another man positioned over him. The man standing over Trudy pointed the gun and shot at her. Then the man at the top of the driveway shot Mickey.

Goodwin's Defense attorney, on cross-examination, tried to attack both witnesses as to their ability to see both Trudy and Mickey at the same time. The Defense tried to infer this was part of a Hollywood plot and asked questions to try to discredit this theory. Although these witnesses were testifying to events they observed 18 years earlier, both seemed to handle the cross-examination well.

When it came time for Dr. Lance Jordan to testify in court, the Defense was ready for him. He was a psychology instructor at Pasadena City College who was Mickey's neighbor and friend. His testimony was as follows:

"There was silence for 15 to 20 seconds, and all of a sudden, I heard Mickey Thompson screaming, 'Please don't hurt my wife! Please don't hurt my wife!' screaming, several times. Then I heard another series of gunshots. Then I grabbed my .357 magnum gun out of a drawer. Then I saw two African American men, wearing sweat suits, riding bicycles down Thompson's back driveway. I screamed at them. I yelled, "'Stop!" They didn't look in my direction as they continued on. I took a shot at them with the .357 magnum from my home. Using that gun, at 6 o'clock in the morning, it was extremely loud. Nobody looked up at me.

Afterward, I saw Trudy lying at the other end of the driveway with blood coming out of her head, and her eyes were wide open. She appeared to be dead."

On cross-examination, Defense attorney Saris asked him why he shot at the men when he had not seen them committing a crime. He bristled at the suggestion that it was unnecessary. Undoubtedly, jurors and others in the courtroom had to wonder as to the wisdom of shooting at two black men running away. Attorneys are sensitive to the differing beliefs in America over the Second Amendment issues (Right to Bear Arms) and tend to tread lightly in this area. Defense attorney Saris's implication that Dr. Jordan was misusing his firearm was an area many attorneys would try to avoid. She continued her cross-examination about whether he was an unbiased witness. She got him to acknowledge that he had appeared on the TV show of 'Unsolved

Mysteries' and narrated an account of the crime that included details that he himself had not observed. Whether he had embellished some of the facts was made an issue that the jury would have to grapple with.

The prosecutors spent considerable time putting on witness after witness explaining all the business dealings and lawsuits between the two men. The key witness was Phillip Bartenetti, who, without a doubt, knew the business dealings of these two business titans better than anyone. He explained how Mickey's company, Mickey Thompson Entertainment Group, joined with Goodwin's company, Stadium Motorsports Corp. Entertainment Specialties, Inc., forming the joint venture called Super Cross Motorcycle Events.

Bartenetti was the man who knew everything about the partnership venture. He was able to go through dozens of business documents and explain to the jury what they meant and how they illustrated the various lawsuits over the $500,000. Then he led the jury down the long tortured road that Mickey went down, trying to collect on the judgment. This was all necessary to establish the lengths that both men went through over these lawsuits. Since Goodwin lost at every step of the way, the prosecution wanted the jury to understand that this was the basis for Goodwin's motive to kill the Thompsons.

The prosecutor, Pat Dixon, with his navy blue Brooks Brothers fitted suits, exuded the LA Law look of a senior partner. Phillip Bartenetti projected the professional look of a Wall Street banker conversing about business deals of the highest order at an exclusive country club. These two men made a dynamic duo, projecting confidence that they knew what they were talking about. Since the business transactions were complex and written in legalese, there was no way that the jurors could possibly grasp all the nuances of this high-power business dealing. It was so important that jurors reach the conclusion that these two men knew what they were talking about and accept it as a business fact. Even the Defense, on cross-examination, tried to question certain documents, but they weren't able to make any inroads.

There were several other similar witnesses that the prosecution called who explained more of the commercial transactions. After a while, several of the jurors looked as though they would have preferred having a root canal than hearing more business testimony. However, several of the male jurors seemed to be fascinated in hearing about the inside operation as to how the real wheelers and dealers operate. The younger men, most likely, thought they could gain some inside tips on how to run a business. Others might have thought they should have received college credits for an MBA degree after sitting through all this testimony about business.

After five weeks, it seemed that the trial was dragging on with the parade of so many witnesses. The Defense was waiting for the prosecution to call their Ace witness, Gail Humphrey (pseudonym), who would testify that Goodwin had confessed to her about killing the Thompsons. The investigators had learned about Gail when Goodwin was being prosecuted for the fraudulent loan for the sailboat. Gail had permitted Goodwin to live with her in Aspen, Colorado. She was the one who said that Goodwin came into her room quite excited and showed her a videotape of one of the Unsolved Mysteries shows about the Thompson killings. As stated earlier, she alleged that he said to her, "Look what I've done and what I got away with." Goodwin couldn't 'curb his enthusiasm.' It was as though he wanted to impress Gail, or possibly illustrate to her not to mess with him because he was capable of killing. They continued to live together until there was a serious falling out in which she accused Goodwin of harming her.

These types of witnesses are like gifts that prosecutors can only dream about. Here she would come in and testify that Goodwin had confessed to her. This certainly would solidify a guilty verdict for the prosecution. (Throughout life, everyone learns there is no such thing as a 'free lunch.') Sometimes witnesses come with baggage that forces a prosecutor to show restraint as to who they call to the witness stand.

Gail had some emotional issues that might affect her credibility. Defense attorney Saris made it known that if the DA called her as a witness, she would introduce hospital records showing that this witness had been treated for mental illness. This would be introduced to attack her credibility as a witness. The prosecutors had to weigh how much harm would be done to their overall case if they tried to use her as a witness. So much of a trial is the attorney attempting to earn the jurors' trust. If the prosecution used her, would the jurors have less trust in the rest of the prosecution's case? In some circles, one would say that Defense counsel Saris had the prosecutors 'by the balls' and she could twist them to make it very painful for them.

At the last minute, Alan Jackson stood up in open court and announced that the 'People Rest their case.' The prosecutors weren't going to roll the dice; they were going to hold'em so the jury would never hear about Goodwin's confession to Gail Humphrey. Immediately afterward, the most disappointed person was the Defense attorney, Elena Saris, who had been waiting so patiently to pull the carpet out from under the prosecutors. These are the contests that are played out behind the scenes between attorneys. There is no right or wrong answer, just a gut feeling by the DA that the risk of putting Gail on the stand to get in Goodwin's confession wasn't worth the potential harm to the prosecutors' credibility.

CHAPTER 36. DEFENSE EVIDENCE AT TRIAL

Although Defense attorney Saris would have loved to cross-examine Gail Humphreys, it was now her turn to move on and call her list of witnesses. It appeared that Goodwin was dictating which witnesses would be called. He seemed insistent on calling the Sheriff's Homicide detectives, not to see what they could add to his Defense, but to try to humiliate them over mistakes they may have made in conducting their investigation.

The prosecutor had decided that Det. Lillienfeld wouldn't be called as a witness by them, since he had mistakenly testified that the guns owned by Goodwin matched the type that had been used in the Thompson shooting. It turned out that Goodwin's 9mm had an opposite twist and couldn't have been one of the murder weapons. Although Det. Lillienfeld had nothing to add to the Defense, they called him as a Defense witness to show how the Sheriff's Department had done a shoddy investigation and that they had a vendetta against Goodwin. The Defense had little to gain by calling Det. Lillienfeld except trying to demean him in front of a packed courtroom.

Goodwin had such a strong dislike for Det. Lillienfeld that he couldn't see that this tactic was ineffective since Det. Lillienfeld projected a professional image in front of the jurors. Defense counsel Saris asked the following question:

"So is it fair to say all the witnesses who you talked to embellished their testimony when they came to the preliminary hearing?"

She tried to imply that the Sheriff's Department was being pressured by Mickey's sister to bring charges against Goodwin. He was asked why he took the case to the Orange County DA's Office. There was no way that long-time Homicide Detective Lillienfeld was going to get tripped up on the Defense's little zingers. His answers were crisp, and this gave him an opportunity to explain why things were done a certain way.

Saris called the original detective, Michael Griffs, and tried to imply that he and the other detectives had done a shoddy job in investigating the double homicide. She discussed the lack of testing of Trudy's fingernails. Then there were the missing orange peels: where could they be? Eventually, the old-time, retired detective said he had nothing further to add and left it at that. Undoubtedly, Goodwin received a sense of satisfaction that he could try to disgrace the detectives who had doggedly pursued him for years.

The Defense was holding an ace that the prosecution couldn't do anything about. There was a 13-year gap between the Johnses' observations of Goodwin to the time of their identification of him at the live lineup. Personal experience has taught most people that over time people are less likely to correctly identify a person. Saris knew if she played this card right, the prosecution's case would look like a 'house of cards collapsing.' She knew that the Public Defender's Office had an ID expert they used in Robbery cases when eyewitness identification is crucial to those cases.

The one witness considered the best ID expert was Kathy Pezdek, a Claremont Graduate University psychologist and associate dean who held herself out as an expert on human memory. Saris had her testify in front of the jury as to her opinion of the Johnses' identification of Goodwin, 13 years after their brief encounter. This expert witness testified that after reviewing the identification of the Johnses, in her professional opinion a misidentification is very likely under these circumstances. She cited a study that found that mistakes in identification increase from 65% correct after one week to 50% correct after three months and then dropped to 10% correct after 11 months. She said in her opinion that the likelihood of accurately recalling a human face 13 years after a brief encounter was zero.

The defense had scored a bullseye on the Johnses' identification. Next, the Defense moved on to plant the seed of doubt that the shooting was the result of a robbery. The Defense called Rene LeConte (pseudonym), an investigator who took a report in 1988 about the Thompson murders. It stated that one of Mickey's employees claimed Mickey had said that he had taken possession of $250,000. However, at trial, the employee couldn't confirm details of the conversation, and the entire issue seemed to fizzle out. But the defense wasn't disappointed, since they only wanted to make the suggestion that it could have been a robbery.

Through various means, the Defense was able to get before the jury the fact that Hollywood had run the Thompson story six times on ***America's Most Wanted***, several times on ***Unsolved Mysteries***, and ***48 Hours,*** the latter broadcasting two one-hour specials. This was all presented to the jurors and later, in the Defense's Argument, they would tie it all together.

After a seven-week trial, the moment of truth arrived, which was whether Goodwin would take the witness stand and tell his story to the jury. The prosecution had worked day and night preparing the most penetrating questions to ask Goodwin if he decided to testify. Everyone who ever came in contact with Goodwin knew that he had a giant ego and he truly believed he was smarter than anyone else. What the defense had to decide was whether the jury would see him as a confident, brilliant businessman, or would they see him as an arrogant control freak who would do anything to prove he was a winner.

This was a tough decision for the Defense because Goodwin could be charming and articulate. Defense attorney Saris realized that if she called him, the prosecution was ready to introduce Goodwin's prior felony conviction for fraudulent activity. Usually, the jurors never know about a defendant's criminal history because the law believes that a defendant should be judged on the facts of his or her present case and the jury should not be influenced by his or her past criminal history.

The exception to this rule is when the defendant testifies; then the defendant's criminal background is relevant to determine his or her credibility. Saris didn't want the jurors to have a negative impression of Goodwin, so his taking the witness stand had a major downside. He could tell the jury that he was a mere scapegoat for a vendetta conducted by the Thompson family members. He could admit that there were business differences between the two men, but they were within weeks of working it out. But on the other hand, the Defense attorneys could recognize that their client had a 'hair trigger' and could easily explode. The two prosecutors were the best of the best, especially when it came to cross-examining defendants. Their penetrating questions could turn into mind games, and Goodwin couldn't resist doing whatever was necessary to appear to be the winner, even if it meant convicting himself.

At the very last minute, Goodwin's Defense attorney, Saris, announced that the defendant, Goodwin, had agreed to waive his right to take the witness stand. The judge wanted to make sure Goodwin agreed, and obtained a personal waiver from him. Then the judge announced that the court would conduct a field trip to the crime scene the next day. The jurors seemed to perk up on hearing that news.

CHAPTER 37. JURY FIELD TRIP

Thursday, December 14, 2006, was another uneventful day in history, except for the fact that on a chilly, breezy day in 1903, the Wright brothers made their first attempt to fly the Wright Flyer at Kitty Hawk, North Carolina. That certainly changed the way we travel. In the Goodwin case, it was a cold, blustery day for a Jury Field Trip to the crime scene in Bradbury. In order for a judge to approve a jury field trip, many factors come into play. First, the court has to get the permission from the party who owns the property to permit such a visit. Of course, a judge can order that an owner must comply, but it is easier to have their cooperation.

The court had to arrange the transportation for the jurors and the court staff from the courthouse to travel to the crime scene. Since the court bailiffs are employees of the Sheriff's Department, it is generally up to the Sheriff's Transportation Bureau to provide the transportation vehicles. On some occasions, large custody buses are used; however, they lack the amenities that jurors are accustomed to. The bars on the bus windows and all the graffiti scratched into the seats can have a chilling effect on jurors. Especially, on warm days, the body odor of the prisoners continues to permeate the entire bus, making for a less-than-pleasant traveling experience.

If possible, the Sheriff will try to line up several nine-passenger vans, which might not be too stylish but the aroma is an improvement over the Sheriff's buses. In the Goodwin case, the sheriff was able to procure two white vans that were able to accommodate all the jurors plus alternates. Each van had a bailiff assigned to it to make sure the judge's instructions were strictly adhered to.

Before the vans left the courthouse, additional Sheriff's deputies were sent in advance to secure the area so the media and bystanders wouldn't interfere with the jurors' viewing. One of their jobs was to transport the large poster charts that were exhibits in the trial. At the crime scene, these exhibits were placed next to what they depicted. This would permit the jurors to compare what the crime scene looked like then and now. Several of the charts showed the photos of Trudy's body, and these were displayed by leaning them against the wall at the entrance to the driveway. Other charts regarding the location of Mickey's body were placed against the garage door.

The DA's Office was a fast learner as to how jury field trips can be a devastating disaster for the prosecution. During the famous O.J. Simpson jury field trip, the prosecutors were caught off guard by the shenanigans of Johnny Cochran and his crew. When Judge Lance Ito had the jurors transported by bus to O.J.'s house on Rockingham Avenue in Brentwood, California, the interior of the house had been redecorated. On the staircase going up to the master bedroom, there had been dozens of photos on the wall of young ladies seemingly falling out of their bikinis. Apparently, when O.J. was a judge of a bikini contest in Hawaii, he was rewarded with photos of all the hot contestants. These photos did add to the bachelor pad décor of the house after Nicole and the children had moved out.

However, on the afternoon of the jury viewing, all those photos had been replaced with photos of O.J.'s mother, family, and his young children. So, as the jurors were being escorted up the stairs, they were able to enjoy O.J.'s wholesome family photos. When the jurors arrived at the top of the staircase, they were met by the gigantic Norman Rockwell painting of a little black girl walking to school with a U.S Marshal during the civil rights movement. That painting was nowhere to be found in the house on the night of the murders. No one could explain how it got on the wall that the jurors couldn't miss. Also, somehow magically, several large pictorial books of Dr. Martin Luther King, Jr. were perfectly placed on coffee tables throughout the house. After the jury viewing was over, the prosecutors immediately looked at the crime scene photos of the house, and none of those coffee tables had any such books.

Afterward, the DA's realized they had been hoodwinked by Johnny and crew. They objected to Judge Ito, but it was deemed too late and nothing could be done to inform the jurors that O.J.'s house had been significantly changed. It was like, how do you unring a bell? So, lesson learned, and when the subject came up about a jury field trip in the Goodwin case, the prosecutors weren't going to be caught flat-footed. They had their exhibit charts ready to transport to the crime scene so the jurors could see what it really looked like on the morning of the murders.

Since the viewing of the crime scene was a part of the court proceedings, the court clerk and court reporter had to be present to record everything for the record. The defendant has a right to be present, which creates a mammoth security issue for the bailiff. When a defendant is in custody during a jury field trip, he or she has to be in handcuffs or surrounded by several burly Sheriff's deputies. Most Defense attorneys believe that it is harmful to the defendant's image when he or she has to be guarded so closely. That may have been the reason why Goodwin waived his right to be present at the jury field trip. For the judge and bailiff, this was a major relief since they could move about more freely and direct their attention to the actual viewing.

At the appropriate time, the two Sheriff's vans drove up to the top of the Thompson's driveway, and the jurors eagerly exited. They were ready to stretch their legs, possibly because they were not used to feeling like sardines in a Sheriff's van. The judge tried to focus the jurors' attention to various sites that they could see at the top of the driveway. This worked for a limited time, but since jurors are naturally curious, some wanted to play super sleuths on their own. Within minutes, one of the jurors squatted down where Mickey's body had been and tried to get a view of where Trudy's body had been at the bottom of the driveway. Other jurors went over to him to see what he had discovered on his own.

While at the top of the hill, the judge pointed out the garage Trudy had backed out of. Naturally, the jurors were curious what it looked like inside. One of them raised his hand and asked if they could go into the garage to look around. The judge wanted to accommodate them but realized that the house and garage were owned by a different family and had a lot of their own property in the garage. The judge advised them that it was permissible to open the garage door but not to go inside. This little exercise seemed to satisfy the jurors' interest in the garage, so the judge gave them a few more minutes and then had everyone taken down to the entrance of the driveway where they were shown the location of Trudy's body. The judge, at that location, pointed out where the Triarsi house was located across the little valley on the other side of Woodlyn Lane. This was a critical issue as to whether Allison Triarsi could actually see what she testified to. All the jurors were sandwiched back into the vans and driven up to where the Triarsis had lived at the time, so they could look down at the Thompson's driveway.

The judge instructed all the jurors that each of the vans would drive by Dr. Jordan's house, which would be on their right, and then they would continue to traverse the country lanes to the south gate. There they stopped and squeezed themselves out of the vans to view the area where witness Wilma Johnson said she saw the two bicyclist ride out of the south gated entrance and dart across Royal Oaks Road in front of her. To illustrate the curiosity of jurors, one of them asked if they could walk across the road to see the bike path where the bicyclists had disappeared. The judge had to make one of those legal executive decisions. She looked at the Sheriff's deputies and asked if they could stop traffic so the jurors could safely walk across the road. It's amazing as to the power of a judge on a field trip. She was able to stop traffic with her command, or as some motorist might exclaim, she caused unnecessary traffic congestion.

The jurors, after looking at the bike path, were escorted back to the vans. One of the jurors asked if they could drive by the Johnses' house. The house was several blocks away, so it would be easy to do. Then the Defense attorney, out of the presence of the jurors, vigorously objected to such a viewing. It wasn't clear what the basis for the objection was, but possibly the Defense didn't want to overemphasize the importance of the Johnses' testimony. The prosecution had no objection to such a viewing. The judge realized that she had to make another totally discretionary decision. Judges must make rulings on objections by counsel. She tried to come up with a compromise and ruled the vans were permitted to drive by, but the jurors would not be permitted to get out of the vans. The vans slowly drove by the Johnses' house as the jurors gazed out the windows.

Was the jury viewing a plus or minus for either side? Only time would tell, and the prosecutors seemed pleased that they hadn't been broadsided, as in the O.J. Simpson jury field trip. Nonetheless, prosecutors always get nervous when various jurors start to overanalyze the case by playing 'Monday morning quarterbacks.' Sometimes jury viewing can divide a jury into different camps: those who saw certain things and those who didn't see.

CHAPTER 38. DA'S ARGUMENT

After a lengthy trial with so many witnesses, the jurors felt relieved when it is time for Argument. Every attorney who went to law school did it because they loved to argue and have people listen to them. Attorneys like the challenge of trying to persuade someone of their point of view. As much as attorneys like to argue, the real issue is how effective are they at arguing. Merely standing in front of a jury and arguing isn't what is important. The true test is how much knowledge one can convey to the jurors. Also, the Argument has to be in a format that is persuasive and memorable.

Both the prosecution and defense recognize the importance of using a PowerPoint presentation to impart the information to the jurors. Prosecutor Alan Jackson had mastered the use of PowerPoint, and in discussing the facts and law with the jury. He had great verbal skills, and he used his slide presentation more as a backdrop to reinforce what he was saying.

When the judge announced it was time for the prosecution's Argument, Alan stood up from his chair and turned to look at the jurors. He walked toward the jury box but moved slightly to the side so all the jurors could see what was on the projection screen, which was the image of Goodwin. Alan looked the jurors in the eye and said the following:

"This case is about a man with a giant ego who didn't like to lose. Mickey Thompson had beaten him in their business dealings. Michael Goodwin didn't like to be a loser, and this outraged him since he had always been a winner."

At that point, he clicked to his next slide, which showed a photo of both Mickey and Trudy with their German Shepherd between them. Alan then stated the obvious.

"On March 16, 1988, at 6:05 a.m., Michael Goodwin had assassins execute Mickey Thompson and his wife as he said he would.

That evidence alone suggests Michael Goodwin is guilty. That evidence alone suggests the ominous nature of this crime.

If Mickey Thompson was forced to watch his wife die, this was the most personal, and brutal attack."

With that introduction, Alan was ready to go to work explaining the law to the jurors so they would understand what they had to do. Unfortunately, Alan needed the jurors to understand all the numerous legal concepts they had to consider and use in order to reach a verdict. He started out by explaining there were two murder charges, one for each victim. Next, he said that they would have to consider two Special Circumstances, one being Multiple Murders and the other being Lying in Wait.

He further took the jurors through the elements of Murder, followed by the types of Murders. The next step involved how to arrive at First Degree Murder. There are several ways: Deliberate and Premeditated, Felony Murder, or Murder by Specific Means, such as when there is Lying in Wait. What was causing Alan to get so many puzzled looks from the jurors was the fact he was referring to using Lying in Wait for two purposes. One was for proving the Special Circumstances and the other to establish First Degree Murder.

This was where Alan inserted the facts that the jurors had heard from Elizabeth Devine, the criminalist, about the orange peels in the tall brush. Alan said that the orange peelings showed that the killers had time to wait for the Thompsons to leave for work. He listed the three components for Lying in Wait, which included concealment, watchful waiting, and finally, a surprise attack.

Alan related his analogy how the jurors are to use their own 'common sense' in applying the law to the facts. He said that he calculated the average age of the jurors was about 40 years old, and if you multiply that by 12 jurors you have, between all of you, 480 years of common sense. Some of the older jurors smiled when he used this since they were flattered to be listed in the 40-year-old category.

The next legal concept that needed to be addressed was the issue of 'Aiding and Abetting.' The prosecution needed the jurors to understand that anyone who takes part in a murder is guilty of the crime, even if they don't pull the trigger or even if they aren't present. Alan used the football analogy that even the Offensive Coordinator receives a Super Bowl ring, regardless of the fact that he never stepped foot on the field during the game. Then he went on to say that Goodwin's scoping out the area, two days before the murders, was sufficient to show that he was involved in the murders, even though he wasn't there on the day of the shootings.

This seemed a little risky for the prosecution to use such an analogy, since it assumed that all the jurors were going to believe that the Johnses' identification was correct after 13 years. However, Alan moved on to his next topic quickly, which involved the issue of an alibi. This was a risky area for the prosecution, since they, by law, can't mention anything about the fact that the defendant didn't testify. Since this can result in reversible error, most prosecutors will avoid this area in their Argument. What is permissible for the prosecution to mention is that the defendant could have called certain witnesses besides himself to provide himself with an alibi.

In order to prevent an Appellate Court reversal, the prosecutor used the following story to make it clear what he was talking about. Alan said, "If I were accused of committing a crime right at this moment, I would call everyone in this room as a witness to prove where I was." As Alan looked at the court clock, he added, "At 11:10 a.m." He was cautious to stay away from inferring the jury could consider the fact that he didn't testify as evidence of guilt.

Next, on explaining the law, he touched on the 'Law of Conspiracy,' which requires the parties to have an agreement that there was an overt act done in furtherance of the conspiracy. Alan realized that this is an area where the attorney can lose the jury. He flashed the esoteric law of Conspiracy on the screen so the jurors could see how confusing it was. Then he summarized it by saying that all the conspirators don't have to meet together, but everyone who is a part of the conspiracy is equally guilty. Then Alan finished by discussing the legal concepts of 'Reasonable Doubt' and the use of 'Circumstantial Evidence.' It was questionable how much the jurors understood after all the legal discussion.

At that moment, Alan stepped back from the jury box and laid down the stack of jury instructions on the counsel table. This was his 'pregnant pause' before he moved into the meaty chunk of his Argument. He clicked his computer and the bold word "THE EVIDENCE" appeared, followed by the words, 'THE MOTIVE,' and then

"THE LAWSUIT & JUDGMENT." Then, slowly fading into focus on the screen was a photo of Goodwin with the court judgment listing the amount of $793,069.40, which included the interest and attorney fees.

Alan then used his PowerPoint slide to fill up the entire screen, listing all the losses Goodwin suffered during all the lawsuits. This was where the magic of a computer slide show can have a significant impression on the jurors. The jurors could view all the losses and see what impact this would have on a person who doesn't like losing. The natural conclusion would be the strong dislike for the person who caused him to suffer all those losses.

Alan started going through each and every threat the prosecution had proved at trial. There were 13 slides with the wording of each threat with the witnesses' name and date. Alan went through each one, showing the vitriolic hatred Goodwin had for Mickey. A few of the threats are as follows:

"I'm too smart; they'll never catch me. Fucking Thompson is destroying me! I'm gonna take him out." (Jan. 1988)

"I'm gonna take Thompson out. I'll never get caught." (Jan. 1988)

"Mickey Thompson has to die for me to get out of this mess. They can't touch me." (late 1980s)

"I got fucked royally by Mickey Thompson. I want to get even with him." (Nov. 1987)

"Before Mickey Thompson gets my money, I'll have him wasted." (Jan. 1988)

"If I lose the lawsuit, I'll kill him. The hit could be done for $20,000." (1984)

"Don't worry honey. I'm gonna take care of him." (Fall 1987)

"He doesn't know who he's fucking with. Mickey Thompson is fucking dead!" (early 1988)

"I'll kill that motherfucker! I'll kill that motherfucker." (late 1987)

"It will cost me $500 & a motorcycle to have you taken out. And I will take you out" (early 1986)

"I'm going to hurt you. I'm going to hurt your family. (Jan. 1988)"

The prosecution wanted the jurors to consider all these threats and take it to the logical conclusion that Goodwin wanted Mickey to suffer a worse fate than what he had suffered. Since Mickey thought the world of his wife, forcing him to watch her being executed would certainly cause him excruciating pain. The prosecution wanted the jurors to believe that Goodwin was diabolical enough to do this. The jury had not heard any witness testify to hearing Goodwin say that he killed them for that reason. If the DA's had called Gail Humphreys, who claimed that Goodwin had bragged how he killed the Thompsons, then that would have been proved. However, the prosecutors thought her testimony came with too much baggage, so they didn't call her. So the prosecutors tried to use the crime scene witnesses to supply the basis for their scenario of the killings.

They used Allison Triarsi to set the stage, in which she testified that she could see Trudy at the bottom of the driveway and Mickey at the top. This established that Mickey had a clear, straight, unobstructed view of Trudy. Allison said she heard Mickey yelling, "Please don't hurt my wife!" Moments later, she saw the gunman standing next to Trudy, shooting her several times. After that, more shots were directed at Mickey.

All of what Allison said was corroborated by Dr. Jordan, the neighbor on the north side, who claimed to have heard Mickey screaming, "Please don't hurt my wife." Where the bodies were found supported Allison's statement that a gunman had been next to Mickey at the top of the driveway and the other gunman was at the bottom with Trudy. Also, the ballistics supported her in that the shell casings were from two separate guns and were found in the general area of both bodies. Lastly, the coroner's opinion supported that the shots to the head were the last and fatal ones.

The prosecution's scenario of the killing was certainly supported by facts that the hit men purposely kept Mickey alive to witness his wife's death. However, the prosecution had to be careful that some of the jurors might not be convinced beyond a 'Reasonable Doubt' or that the killings occurred in that order. Goodwin would still be guilty of the murders, even if the plan was to shoot and kill Mickey and kill any witnesses at the scene. Since Trudy was a witness to Mickey's killing, she had to be disposed of as well. Alan realized he had to back away from the diabolical scenario to allow the jurors more flexibility to interpret the evidence at the crime scene.

It was now time for the prosecution to counter the defense's attack on the Johnses' identification 13 years later. Since Dr. Kathy Pezdek had testified just a couple of days earlier, her testimony was still on the minds of the jurors. Alan cited Pezdek's words that after 11 months there is a zero chance that someone could identify a person. Since it was only a short time before Christmas, Alan used a folksy comparison. He said to the jurors, "My little brother has been away at school for the past 11 months, so when he arrives home at Christmas no one in the family will recognize him, according to Dr. Pezdek."

The jurors seemed to be weighing in their minds what Alan had just said. After letting the jurors think about it, he said that obviously other factors come into play, such as the manner in which you meet that person. If it was a long time you knew the person or if it had been a serious event, such as thinking they might be child molesters or using binoculars to look at a school. Alan had made his point, and he didn't want the jurors to dwell on the Johnses' identification.

The next area Alan wanted to address was Goodwin's 'Flight' after the crime to show 'Consciousness of Guilt.' In order to prove this to the jury, he had to refer to dozens of documents and contracts. This is where Alan heavily relied on his PowerPoint presentation to be front and center. His first slide had a title at the top with the words "Escape" and "Purchased a Yacht." On the right was a photo of a similar yacht that Goodwin had purchased. On the left was the loan approval document for the yacht, in his wife's name, with the date of March 10, 1988, which was six days before the murders.

The prosecutor's next slide showed documents that Goodwin and his wife were dumping assets in order to get money transferred out of the country. One slide showed their house was placed in escrow on March 18, 1988, just two days after the murders. Then the prosecutor used a summary slide showing the sale of their investments and the placing of the money in two banks that wired that money to Barclay's bank in the Cayman Islands. The rest of their money was converted to Krugerrands and transferred out of the country.

Almost a week of testimony was distilled into three slides showing how Goodwin had been planning to leave the country around the time Mickey and Trudy were murdered. Then the prosecutor clicked to the next slide and showed the law on 'Flight After a Crime.' The wording on the slide stated, **"The escape of a person after a crime may be considered by the jury in determining guilt."** Since the defendant didn't testify and there wasn't any testimony before the jury explaining any other reason for the sudden move to the Caribbean for the next year or so, the inference was evidence of "Consciousness of Guilt."

Alan knew that the Defense was going to try to suggest that the murders were the result of a 'robbery gone bad.' He said that the Defense wanted to make something out of the fact that the shooters were wearing white backpacks to take money and jewelry. The Defense tried to plant the seed that Mickey had received a large amount of cash that he might have been storing in several safes he had in the garage and house.

Alan said that none of this made sense since burglars would wait for the occupants of a house to leave before they would break in to steal. If this had been a robbery of Mickey, why wouldn't they take his wallet, which had several thousand dollars in it? As to Trudy, why wouldn't a robber take some of her jewelry, which was worth thousands of dollars? This was the easiest part of the prosecutors' Argument by claiming that the Defense was using Robbery as a 'Red Herring' to have the jurors take their eyes off the ball.

The prosecutor clutched his papers together firmly and said in closing:

"To say this is anything other than a perfectly planned, perfectly orchestrated, perfectly choreographed execution, does violence to logic, folks."

The DA finished with his PowerPoint presentation with a slide displaying the following words:

GOODWIN: I'm going to hurt you. I'm going to hurt your family.

MICKEY: Please don't hurt my wife.

TRUDY EXECUTED. MICKEY EXECUTED

The prosecutor ended by saying that **it was as if Goodwin signed his name to this crime**. He then clicked, and with a slow dissolve, the photo of Goodwin appeared looking down on Mickey's and Trudy's dead bodies. The only words on the screen were these:

March 16, 1988

I'll have him wasted.

Alan took one step toward the jurors and in a strong, resolute voice said,

"Your job as jurors is to protect, and seek justice and with all this evidence to find Michael Goodwin Guilty of the murder of Mickey Thompson and Trudy Thompson."

With that, the prosecutor sat down and the screen behind him slowly faded to black.

CHAPTER 39. DEFENSE'S ARGUMENT

At 1:40 p.m., the court was again called to order by the bailiff, and the judge stated the defense may argue. Elena Saris eagerly rose up as though she couldn't wait any longer to tell her side of the story to the jury. Her serious demeanor was illustrated by her steely eyes, framed with her arched eyebrows. Her thin lips projected a voice intent on being heard. She likewise had a PowerPoint slide show, which contained considerable text in all caps making it problematic to read. She came prepared to do battle with the prosecutors. Attacking the prosecution's Argument commenced with her announcement that her client was not guilty of these murders.

Her first point zeroed in on what she called was the Hollywood version of how Mickey Thompson was killed. She exclaimed it was a giant myth not borne out by any real facts. She listed how many times TV programs had depicted the killings as though Mickey was forced to view the execution of his wife. She said the facts from the coroner's testimony showed that Mickey was shot first and killed by a bullet to the head. She kept complaining the DA was trying to change the facts to support their Hollywood version. She explained that where Mickey's body was found he wouldn't have been able to see Trudy at the bottom of the driveway.

She went on to say that since law enforcement couldn't catch the shooters, that there was a feeling that someone must pay for such cold-blooded murders. The idea was to find someone to blame, possibly someone who wasn't very popular.

"Call him a jerk, call him an egomaniac, call him a braggart, but prove what you're alleging, rather than arouse passion and prejudice against this man."

Goodwin certainly had his disputes with Mickey; therefore, he became an easy target to blame. She started to show how the Sheriff's detectives had botched the case. To prove this, she pointed out that the DA didn't even call the original detective in the case. She made it seem that there was a delay of at least 13 years before starting a real investigation into the case.

Attorney Saris criticized the investigation for failing to find a hair on the tape covering the stun gun, which she submitted for DNA testing. She further chided the detectives for not following up on the information from the Johns, which produced eyewitnesses so many years after the events. She mentioned the prosecutor wanted to attack the testimony of Dr. Pezdek, who pointed out how unreliable an identification can be 13 years later.

She moved on from the botched investigation to discuss other explanations for the attacks on the Thompsons, such as Robbery. She initially talked about the shooters having the white canvas bags, which could be used to carry loot. Then she talked about missing valuables from safes that were later found to be open. She glossed over the testimony that the safes were later opened by the investigators, which caused the pry marks on the outside of the safes. She continued to support her

Argument that the shooters weren't hit men, since they had chambered several bullets without firing them. She implied professional hit men wouldn't do that.

Then her attention was directed to the Financial Myth in which Goodwin's Mercedes wasn't taken by Mickey but involved an entirely different person. Further myths were that Mickey took the Rose Bowl contract away from Goodwin. She said that was a myth since no one wanted to use the Rose Bowl as a venue for stadium racing. She continued to explain that Mickey didn't get anything from Goodwin because the assets were in Diane's name. She then switched to the subject of Goodwin going into bankruptcy, and there wasn't anything sinister about that. She said that even the airlines use bankruptcy all the time as a way to reorganize their business. As to purchasing the yacht, that was innocent since Goodwin was a professional underwater photographer. In order to have communication, he had the yacht equipped with a worldwide phone system so he could stay in contact with people, such as his attorney. On several occasions during his Caribbean sailing, Goodwin flew back and forth to Mexico.

The Defense claimed that Goodwin offered to give Mickey the White Rock property for the $795,387 that was owed. She said it was Mickey who turned down the offer and later Diane was able to sell the property for much more than the judgment. By this time it appeared that the Defense Argument had gotten lost in the weeds. Or possibly Goodwin was calling the shots as to what should be argued. The Argument seemed to take on the appearance of Goodwin being smarter than Mickey in that he transferred all his assets to his wife, Diane, who in turn sent them out of the country so Mickey would never be able to take them. The winner is really Michael Goodwin.

Next was sort of a surreal event when the Defense attorney Saris went through a list of all the prosecution witnesses as she showed their names on the screen. One by one, she found something wrong with the testimony of each of them, such as that they had been inconsistent at some time over the years. She criticized witness Kathy Wilton, who had testified she overheard Goodwin telling Mickey that he could have him wasted. Defense counsel said the conversation couldn't have happened since Goodwin wasn't talking to Mickey at that time. It was a tedious process, since a better approach would have been selecting your best ones and concentrating your Argument on them. The less important witnesses' testimony could be summarily discussed not to distract from major witnesses that you want the jurors to remember.

The Defense's Argument was without a doubt protracted and thorough. Elena Saris made sure she covered every possible point. The Sheriff's investigation was referred to as an 18-year witch-hunt for proof against Michael Goodwin. She reminded the jurors the evidence that the DA presented to them was full of 'Reasonable Doubt.' They tried to make you dislike the defendant. Then she went on to explain that the law protects even people who are jerks. Just because you dislike a person isn't a reason to convict him when there is no evidence to connect him to the murders. Saris glanced at her notes and slowly sat down next to her client, who seemed to be pleased with her exhaustive presentation.

The DA had the opportunity to make a short Rebuttal Argument in which the prosecutor addressed several of the issues raised by the Defense. Then it was time for the judge to read the jury instructions to the jurors. As mind-numbing as it was, the jurors listened intently, pretending they understood everything they were being told. Unfortunately, jury instructions are written by attorneys, who use terms that aren't common to the lay jurors. However, it is like religious dogma that legal scholars believe is necessary to provide guidelines for the jurors to follow in order for them to do their job during their deliberations.

CHAPTER 40. VERDICT & SENTENCING

After the judge had read the jury instructions, the jury commenced their deliberation. After four days, in which the jurors continued to go over the evidence trying to reach a verdict, they still needed more time. Since it was getting near to the Christmas holidays, the judge told the jurors to take a break in their deliberation and come back after the first of the year. On Tuesday, January 2, 2007, the jurors reappeared to resume deliberations. It was only two days later that the jurors rang the buzzer, indicating they had reached a verdict.

The courtroom clerk had to play the role of Paul Revere by quickly notifying the attorneys, the news media, and victims' families that the jurors had reached a verdict. This is no easy task, since the attorneys most likely were downtown in their offices. However, within several hours all were assembled in Judge Schwartz small courtroom. There was standing room only, filled with neighboring judges, court staff, and attorneys who just happened to be in the courthouse at the time.

This was truly a big event for the old Pasadena courthouse, since most of the time it is the downtown Criminal Courts Building that handles most of the publicity cases. By the time Judge Schwartz took the bench, the courtroom was so crowded that there was no room for another human body to squeeze in. Old-time court watchers were hoping there was no one from the Fire Marshal's Office in the courthouse. Even on special events, like the verdict in a major case, the court tends to overlook the overcrowding rules.

Thankfully, Colleen Campbell and her husband already had a seat. No one wanted to see Colleen take on a Fire Marshal who might try to bar her from the courtroom. For the past 18 years, Colleen had spent so much of her time trying to get the authorities to prosecute Michael Goodwin. There was no question that Goodwin had a vendetta against Mickey. It was very similar to Colleen's crusade to see that justice was finally served in the death of her brother and sister-in-law. There wasn't anything in the world that was going to prevent Colleen from watching Goodwin's face when the verdict was announced. She had gone through so much disappointment, she had to hope the jury got it right.

Colleen was certain Goodwin was involved, based on what her brother had told her. She was very close to Mickey and generally talked to him three times a week. She remembers he called her three days before his death and said, "I'm worried that Goodwin will try to hurt my wife. Colleen, I'm telling you, the guy's capable of it and I feel it in my bones."

Unfortunately, this statement was inadmissible in court since it was ruled 'hearsay.' It is one of the many oddities of the rules of evidence, which doesn't permit hearsay, unless the defendant, who in this case was Goodwin, can cross-examine the declarant, who was Mickey, who had made the statement. Someone might say it was Goodwin who made it impossible for Mickey to come to court because he was the one who had Mickey killed. As crazy as this may seem, this is the law.

The jurors, all eight women with the four men pulling up the rear, streamed into the courtroom taking their respective seats. One could feel the tension in the courtroom. Those in the audience could see Colleen sitting upright, ramrod straight, with a serious expression on her face. One could see she was wearing the St. Christopher medal her brother wore during his races. This was Mickey's good luck charm that had protected him throughout his racing career. Did the St. Christopher medal still have some good luck in it?

Goodwin was seated at counsel table with his attorney, Elena Saris. He looked tense and appeared to have a forced smile on his face. Within minutes, he would learn his fate. He might be a free man walking out of the courtroom doors, laughing in Colleen's face for all she had done over 18 years to see him convicted. Or, he might learn that he would be spending the rest of his life in a prison cell listening to the clang of metal doors closing behind him.

There are life-defining moments, and this was certainly one of them. The judge asked the jury foreperson if the jury had arrived at a verdict. The foreperson stood up and stated, "We have, Your Honor." Thereupon he handed the verdict forms to the bailiff, who in turn gave them to the judge, who reviewed all the paperwork. This was the moment where everyone in the courtroom was looking at the judge to show some expression. Does she look surprised? Does she look frustrated? Unfortunately, judges must take a course in how to learn not to show any emotion in their faces or body movements. Judge Schwartz had to realize everyone in the courtroom was staring at her, but she gave no clue what was on the verdict forms.

It was apparent the judge wasn't going to reveal the results of the verdicts. She placed everything in order, stretched out her arm, and handed everything to the courtroom clerk to read the verdicts. This is the one moment the courtroom clerk becomes the center of everyone's attention. She cleared her throat and said with a loud, officious voice, "As to count one, the jury finds the defendant Michael Goodwin **GUILTY** of the murder of Mickey Thompson." Everyone's eyes focused on Goodwin, who put his head down and shook it several times, audibly saying, "No, no, I didn't do it." He didn't seem to be listening to the clerk read another GUILTY verdict as to Trudy's murder. The jury found both special allegations to be true.

The jurors were willing to talk afterward with the attorneys. They said that their first ballot was nine for guilty, one for not guilty and two undecided. However, what was most interesting was that the jurors indicated that they were certain, from the beginning, they would reach a verdict. All they had to do was reread the jury instructions, and when they finished all 12 jurors were for Guilty. When asked what evidence they found most useful, as a group they said it was not one witness or piece of evidence but the totality of all the evidence.

As Colleen sat stoically waiting for the entire verdict to be read, tears of joy, or tears of relief, streamed down her cheeks. When it was all over, Colleen left the courtroom with her husband and other family members and friends and they all congregated in the front of the courthouse. The news media asked her what was her reaction to the verdict. Colleen said, "I knew I would see justice done in the deaths of my brother and his wife. But I didn't think it would take two decades and that I'd be 74 years old." Then she immediately turned her attention to handing out fliers with the composite sketches of the two bicycle-riding gunmen. She said, "We still want these people. They're killers. We got one out of three, but we got the main one today." Obviously, Colleen couldn't quite end her crusade to get them all. However, she was pleased to get the big fish.

When the media was able to speak to Goodwin's Attorney, Elena Saris, she indicated that the Defense was very disappointed with the verdict. She reiterated part of her Argument in that the prosecution had no killers, no plan, no meeting, no weapon, no phone calls, no payout, and they had absolutely nothing. It appears she may have been overlooking the 70 witnesses who testified and over 100 exhibits that illustrated the evidence.

The sentencing was put over to March 1, 2007, and was a mere formality. Since the jury had found the Special Circumstance allegations true, Goodwin's sentence was going to be life without the possibly of parole. At the time of sentencing, the first part is called the Victim Impact, at which time anyone from the victim's family can address the court. This was the opportunity for Colleen to say what she had pent up for 18 years, and she said, "Mickey was a true man, an icon, and he is missed beyond what any words could describe. I have received calls from around the world by those distressed and impacted by the murders." Throughout Colleen's statement, Goodwin closed his eyes and shook his head whenever Colleen referred to him as a killer. Before the formal sentencing, the judge asked Goodwin if he had anything to say. Most defendants don't say anything; however, Goodwin took this opportunity to say, "I have condolences for Ms. Campbell. But I can't apologize because I'm not guilty."

When Colleen left the courtroom, she took out a checkered flag and waved it in the air as though it was directed to the heavens, and stated to Mickey and Trudy, "We have finally WON."

What was interesting about the checkered flag is that it symbolizes who is the winner of a race. This entire case was about two headstrong entrepreneurs with giant egos who always wanted to be WINNERS. In this case, Mickey is buried six feet under and Goodwin is living in a prison cell six feet by twelve feet. Unfortunately, in this case, there were NO WINNERS!!

(The following graphic page shows a happy Coleen Campbell and a sad Michael Goodwin.)

Graphic 19

VERDICT

January 2, 2007

VERDICT IN RACING LEGEND'S SLAYING

Goodwin found guilty of Thompson murders

Ex-partner receives life sentence

"It doesn't bring my dad back, but it doesn't let that bastard go."

Sister kept attention on case

Pasadena Courthouse

Coleen Campbell, Mickey's sister had waited 18 years for this day

Mickey Thompson's killer gets 2 life terms

At his sentencing, Michael Goodwin insists he did not plot the murders of the racing legend and his wife in 1988.

CHAPTER 41. EPILOGUE

Michael Goodwin

Goodwin is housed in the High Desert State Prison in Susanville, California, and shares a cell with Eddie. Goodwin had a misunderstanding with another inmate, which resulted in him losing one of his front teeth. Because of that bad experience, he tries to avoid the main yard where the buffed inmates workout. Most of his time is spent in his cell working on his appeal. He uses an electric typewriter in his cell to prepare his motions. In the process, he has turned into a pseudo jailhouse lawyer being sought out by other prisoners to help them with their appeals. His years in jail and prison have caused him to seek religion. Occasionally, his old Motocross buddies visit him, which provides him with an escape back to the good old days when he was the great stadium promoter.

He has convinced a group of visitors that he is an innocent man, falsely convicted. On his behalf, they established a blog site, which Goodwin uses to expound on how unfairly he had been treated by the justice system. He provides audios for his blog by placing phone calls to a person on the outside, who records his diatribes and places them on the internet. This is very similar to a tactic used by another prison inmate who makes phone calls outside which are recorded and placed on the internet. That inmate is better known by the name of Charles Manson, and his recordings are available on the internet as Charlie's songs.

Goodwin's hatred for Colleen Campbell is unrelenting, and he blames his problems on her influence with law enforcement and her one-million-dollar reward, which caused people to make false claims against him. His venom toward Det. Lillienfeld is incessant, and he claims the detective has committed countless perjury violations against him over the years. His strongest contempt is directed against Prosecutor Alan Jackson, whom he accuses of committing fraud during the trial. In 2015, the appellate court upheld his conviction and Goodwin indicated that he would file a habeas corpus based on new evidence that the killings were the result of a robbery.

Alan Jackson

Alan was the 'Wonder Boy' of the DA's Office and rose up the ranks quickly. His career path landed him in Major Crimes Division, where he was paired with the Head Deputy, Pat Dixon, in trying the Goodwin case, and later the duo did the Phil Spector case together. Originally, they got a hung jury, and Alan retried the Goodwin case with Truc Doe, and they were able to obtain a conviction. The Spector case provided a great deal of media attention on Alan, which is a double edged sword. He became the 'media darling,' and they loved his appearances as the handsome prosecutor who was fighting evil and willing to give short sound bites easy to use in numerous legal TV programs.

The danger of being the 'media darling' is the feeling of invincibility. After the Spector case, there was talk of him leaving the DA's Office to be a TV commentator, but he said no thanks and stayed with the DA's Office. Then there was talk that the DA Steve Cooley was going to run for Attorney General, which would open up the DA position. This meant that the Board of Supervisors would select the next DA. Alan recognized this was an opportunity for him to become DA. To some he was considered too young and inexperienced for the appointment; however, he did have a solid base of supporters. Since Cooley lost the AG race, he remained in his position as DA.

Cooley decided not to run for a fourth term as DA. Alan immediately 'threw his hat into the ring' for the DA position. Unfortunately for Alan, Cooley backed his assistant, Jackie Lacey, for the DA position. Alan mounted his own campaign. This was a bruising campaign and Alan, being a Republican, couldn't overcome Jackie Lacey's support from many strong Democrats. He lost the DA race, and after so much name calling during the election, there were reassignments. Alan was relocated to a position that was quite different and wouldn't permit him to try publicity cases as when he was the Assistant Head of Major Crimes Division. This was a hard transition for him, so he quit the DA's Office and went into private practice. This was not a soft landing for Alan, the DA Wonder Boy; nevertheless he has done well in private practice.

Pat Dixon

Over time, Pat took on a higher administrative position overseeing all of the Specialized Prosecutions Divisions. After the election, Pat Dixon was moved to head up Target Crimes, where he remained for a few months and then retired from the DA's Office after a distinguished career trying some of the most complex cases in the Office. He certainly earned a reputation as one of the very top litigators in Southern California. Shortly after retiring, he went into private practice.

Det. Mark Lillienfeld

He continues to work for the Sheriff's Homicide Division. Occasionally he is contacted by the news media and asked why he hasn't run certain DNA tests for Goodwin. He continues to explain that he has placed all the possible DNA evidence into the national database but there have not been any hits. His comment is, what else can he do for Michael Goodwin? Because of his hardnosed attitude and disdain of criminals, the LA Times occasionally will write less-than-flattering articles about the City of the Angeles version of Clint Eastwood's Dirty Harry character. Det. Lillienfeld could care less what the newspaper says about him and he continues to do what he loves to do best and that is catching crooks.

Allison Triarsi

She was only14 when the murders occurred, and she has grown up. She has gone on to be a TV anchor in Minneapolis.

Danny Thompson (Mickey's son)

He has followed his dad into the racing world. Now that he is in his 60s he is doing less racing. His biggest project is to build and race a new Streamliner and to finish the job his father started over 50 years ago. He hopes to break the world speed record at Bonneville Salt Flats. Mickey was able to travel 406.60 mph; however, he couldn't complete the second run because of a broken axle.

Mickey didn't give up and tried again with the Challenger 1 for several more years, but mechanical and weather problems plagued the project. In 1968, Mickey developed a completely different streamliner named the Challenger 2. It was two feet narrower, and it was powered by a pair of Ford SOHC427 engines in tandem, still using four-wheel drive. Mickey had it tested up to 411 mph, but poor weather prevented them from racing it at Bonneville. The following year, Ford Autolite Division ended their sponsorship, so Mickey mothballed this latest streamliner.

There it sat for 20 years until one month before Mickey's death he had a conversation with his son, Danny. Mickey asked his son if he would drive the streamliner Challenger 2 in another attempt to break the world speed record. To Mickey, it was important that a person by the name 'Thompson' be finally listed as the fastest man on wheels. After Mickey's death, Danny lost interest and the project was again mothballed.

Another 25 years went by before Danny arranged a sponsorship of a new project, using the old Autolite streamliner body but updating it and renaming it the Challenger 2.5. This new version would be powered by a pair of Richard Catton-built fuel-injected Chrysler Hemi V-8 engines tied together with a driveshaft and fed with a 30 % mixture of nitro methane.

Everyone kept watching and waiting to see if Danny would be able to set a new world record in his dad's old renovated streamliner, the Challenger 2.5.

In 2016, Danny made another attempt to break the speed record. On August 13, Danny was able to take the new Challenger to a problem-free 411.191 mph, followed by a second run on the next day at 402.348 mph. Averaging the two runs gave Danny the speed record of 406.7. His dad had been able to go 406.6 mph on his first pass on the track before breaking down. What was strange was that Danny only was able to beat his dad by one tenth of one pile per hour and it took 56 years between the two attempts.

Ronald Bowers (THE AUTHOR)

After a 43-year career working for the DA's Office, I finally moved on with my life. I realized I had had the opportunity to work with some incredibly talented people. As a team, we pulled together and accomplished many successful prosecutions on some unbelievably difficult cases. I believe the Mickey and Trudy

Thompson story should be told to illustrate to the public the incredible dedication and unselfish work done by so many in the Criminal Justice System. I am thankful I had the chance to be one of those on the team who helped to close the last chapter in Mickey's life.

My intent in writing this book was to provide the public an opportunity to see how well our court system works, as well as areas where it may need some improvement. I wrote this book from my office, in my home, where I can look out my balcony window and see to the west Mickey's old home in Bradbury. To the east I can see the Hot Rod Hall Of Fame in Pomona, where most of Mickey's racecars are on display.

Every day from my office I am reminded what a legend Mickey had become during his lifetime and even after. There is no question that Goodwin was the **KILLER OF A LEGEND.**

(The following graphic page shows that the Legend of Mickey Thompson still lives on.)

Graphic 20

EPILOGUE

Coleen continues fighting for Victims

Mickey & Trudy Rest in Peace

Goodwin remains at Mule Creek State Prison

AUTHOR'S CONNECTION TO CASE

Everyday author constantly reminded of the legend

MICKEY'S SON

Danny with Mickey's old Challenger
Mickey went 406.6 mph

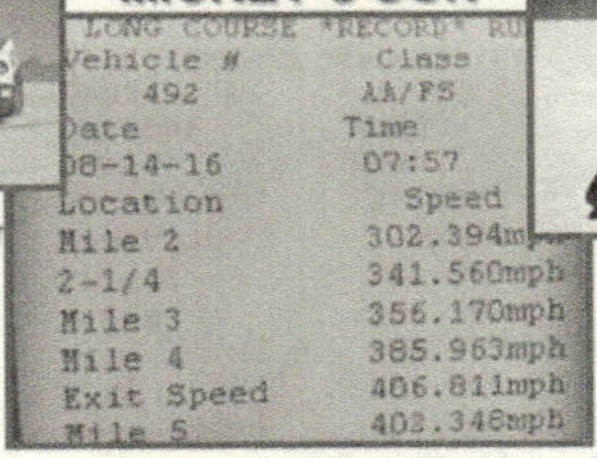

LONG COURSE *RECORD* RU

Vehicle #	Class
492	AA/FS
Date	Time
8-14-16	07:57
Location	Speed
Mile 2	302.394m
2-1/4	341.560mph
Mile 3	356.170mph
Mile 4	385.963mph
Exit Speed	406.811mph
Mile 5	403.348mph

Danny Thompson beat his dad's old speed record by 1/ten of mph 58 years later

Danny's new Challenger
Danny went 406.7 mph

OTHER BOOKS

By Ronald E Bowers

If you enjoyed this book, take a look at my other books I have written.

My tenth book was titled the ***Celebrity Curse.*** This book reviewed the mysterious deaths of celebrities starting with the investigation into **Marilyn Monroe's** death. For over a half a century there has been a growing controversy over her untimely death. Was it an accidental overdose or a suicide? However, over the years more facts have revealed the possibility that she may have been murdered. This book considers all the possibilities trying to separate fact from fiction.

Also included in this book is a behind the scenes look at the case of the enablers in the strange death of **Anna Nicole Smith** which resulted in one of the strangest prosecutions of all times. Further on in the ***Celebrity Curse*** we discuss the mysterious deaths of **John Belushi, Natalie Wood** as well as old-time screen legend **Thelma Todd**. Of course the book wouldn't be complete without including the prosecution of **Michael Jackson's** doctor who was giving the superstar an IV drip of Propofol to assist him in sleeping.

Another aspect of the book ***Celebrity Curse*** is a review of a number to Stalking the Stars cases which include **Madonna, Mel Gibson, Catherine Zeta Jones, John Cusack** and **Steven Spielberg**. Here we discuss the high price of being a celebrity with its loss of privacy and threats to one's life and family members. Without a doubt Stalkers are truly a **CELEBRITY CURSE**.

The next book I wrote was vital to understanding the Criminal Justice System. It was titled the ***Death Penalty Designee.*** Capital Punishment is considered the third hot button issue after Abortion and Gun Control that most people try to avoid discussing. Everyone has some type of emotional attachment either for or against the Death Penalty without truly understanding the purpose or operation of the Death Penalty. The book doesn't take sides but provides the reader with facts and figures to support their positions. The issues are viewed through the eyes of a person, The Death Penalty Designee, who had to make the ultimate decisions of some of the most notorious cases of all times. The book starts with the Tookie Williams case and continues on with the Richard Ramirez (Night Stalker) case followed by the Bitter and Norris case eventually discussing dozens of homicides that everyone has faded memories of.

Another book was the ***Killings on Route 66.*** Part of American history can be told by all who have come west on the old Route 66. This book starts at the very end of Route 66 which is the Santa Monic pier where a number of nefarious cases occurred. Next we travel a few blocks to one of the sites where 10 innocent peoples were slaughtered. We follow Route 66 as it traverses through West Hollywood where Dominick Dunn became inspired to be a celebrated True Crime writer. Further on we come across the most horrific and diabolical double murder of all times in Hollywood. Of course we touch upon Dr. Haing Ngor's Killing Fields this time of LA as we stop for a deadly Dodger's game. It's amazing that not all the carnage on Route 66 came from traffic accidents.

A similar book I wrote was the ***Killers on Mulholland Drive.*** Here I travel down the highway to the Homes of the Stars. I start out relating the sad case of Ennis Cosby who was the victim of a Robbery Gone Bad. Then we weave our way on top of this famous highway to the estate of Marlon Brando where murder raised its ugly head by his son shooting his half-sister's finance while he sat on the sofa watching TV. We can't ignore what happened in his neighbor's house that being Jack Nicholson. That was where Roman Polanski seduced a 14 year old girl and ultimately he became America's most famous fugitive. We examine how this road is Hollywood's Lovers Lane and at times it leads to deadly consequences.

One of my most fascinating books was the ***Old Lady Killers.*** For so many years I have been inundated with homicide cases involving male suspects. There have been a few female murder cases, but they involved women who generally want to knock off their husbands for the life insurance benefits. It is so rare to see a grandmother type committing crime. However, when I had to work on the Sante Kimes case, I couldn't believe how elderly women could be so evil. Next I worked on the case against Helen Golay (76) and Olga Rutterschmidt (74) who made a living caring for the homeless just to run over them to collect the life insurance policies they took out on these men. This book will definitely change your opinion about sweet little old ladies who can be incredibly malicious and wicked.

Another one of my books was the ***Rich Kid Killers of Beverly Hills.*** This book examines the infamous Billionaire Boys Club killing which was the genesis for the Menendez Brothers massacre of their parents. How could rich kids who have experienced the good life and were well educated turn to murder? Most people think that only the poor or less affluent commit crime. Although rich kids' motives to kill are quite different from the poor or gang shootings, however they do occur and can be difficult to solve.

One of my Celerity books was the ***Killing in the Castle.*** Most readers are familiar with Phil Spector, the music producer, who brought us the 'Wall of Sound' and who was accused of killing an actress in his castle/house. However, few people know the true story of how this case labeled the 'Battle of the Experts' resulted in a hung jury. This case illustrates what happens when the defendant has unlimited resource and can hire dozens of Defense attorneys to represent him.

Another book was the ***Killers on the Way to Vegas.*** This book tells the story of two mothers who traveled halfway around the world to find their missing sons. It involved a case that fell between the cracks because the mothers didn't know where their sons were when they went missing. This is a story of how strong two mothers' love can be .They wouldn't accept defeat and ended up on the doorstep of the FBI in Los Angeles. There agents stepped up to the plate to solve one of the most mysterious cases by using a cadaver dog to sniff out a grave in the desert on the way to Vegas.

The LA True Crime series all began with this book the ***Killer at the Door***. It discusses one of those cases in which the DA's Office originally prosecuted the wrong suspect. This book shows how a prosecutor had to right a wrong in order to get the killer at the door. The case has so many twists and turns over a ten year period it took to solve. A long the way this book will introduce the reader to the celebrity world as well as some of the zaniest characters you could ever image.

Made in the USA
Middletown, DE
05 November 2026

36544054R10149